Criminal Convictions

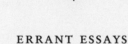

ERRANT ESSAYS
ON PERPETRATORS
OF LITERARY LICENSE

BY

NICOLAS FREELING

David R. Godine · Publisher
BOSTON

First published in 1994 by
DAVID R. GODINE, PUBLISHER, INC.
Horticultural Hall
300 Massachusetts Avenue
Boston, Massachusetts 02115

Library of Congress Cataloging-in-Publication Data

Freeling, Nicolas.
Criminal convictions : errant essays on perpetrators
of literary license / by Nicolas Freeling.—1st ed.
p.   cm.
Contents: Crime and metaphysics—Stendhal—Charles Dickens
—Joseph Conrad—Sir Arthur Conan Doyle—Rudyard Kipling
—Raymond Chandler—Dorothy L. Sayers—Georges Simenon
—Apologia pro vita sua.
1. Detective and mysteries stories—History and criticism.
2. Crime in literature. I. Title.
ISBN 0-87923-973-5 PN3448.D4F7 1994
809.3'872—dc20 94-6430 CIP

FIRST EDITION
Printed and bound in the United States of America

Contents

❦

Introduction   vii

Crime and Metaphysics   3

Stendhal   14

Charles Dickens   26

Joseph Conrad   58

Sir Arthur Conan Doyle   70

Rudyard Kipling   81

Raymond Chandler   110

Dorothy L. Sayers   121

Georges Simenon   132

Apologia Pro Vita Sua   143

w-key, quietly spoken method of Nabokov's beloved Flau-
ert. This approach can be found in English letters—in Trol-
pe surely and Henry James—but most obviously in that
her great Flaubert admirer, Joseph Conrad. If Winnie Verloc
wes a great deal to Emma Bovary how much does Nabokov
we to the high comedy of Mr. Verloc? It is all strangely "un-
nglish," and this is a point one will have to come back to.

The hot or emotionally keyed approach to crime writing is,
be sure, best exemplified in Dickens. Drama is heightened
to melodrama. It has come about, interestingly, that the
ord has acquired a pejorative sense, and one wants to know
hy. *Melos* is Greek for song. Music was used to intensify the
rama. An opera, thus, or a *Missa Solemnis*; plainchant by
onks or Orpheus with his lute. How does this come to have a
ad name, used to define a gaudy or inflated fustian? Styles
hange (the young Laurence Olivier would today sound like
r. Vincent Crummles) but the question goes deeper: we talk
much about death, and especially death by violence, and are
ore and more frightened of meeting it (quite the opposite of
roust's duchess who when asked to give her opinions on Love
id, "I make it, often, but I never talk about it"). How did the
detective story" and all its "mystery" offshoots come to be so
ivolous, so essentially trivial, about death? This was fine in a
oy's adventure story. *Treasure Island* would be nothing with-
ut the slaughter. The boy shudders still (at least, I hope so) at
lver's fearful "Them that dies will be the lucky ones," but the
orpse count is quite acceptable. "But one man of her crew
ive, what put to sea with seventy-five"—par for the course.
ife is so strong in the child; all this death merely stimulates his
nagination. The adult notices that Stevenson was a fine artist:
e deaths are never merely cheap. "Down went Pew with a cry
at rang high into the night." It scorches! While the funda-

Introduction

————————— ❧ —————————

In his *Lectures on Literature* Vladimir Nabokov remarks that
"literature was born on the day when the boy came crying
wolf, wolf, and there was no wolf." (That is, of course, a crime
story.)

"Between the wolf in the tall grass and the wolf in the tall
story," he continues, there is a prism, "a shimmering go-
between," which is the art of literature. The magic of art was in
the shadow of the wolf, the dream of the wolf. It could not be
put better, nor with more concision.

This was in the introduction to his course on some half-
dozen masterpieces of European prose fiction, given to his students at Cornell University in the fifties (collected, since, in
book form, and altogether admirable). I have emphasized "in
the fifties"; he had not yet written *Lolita*, which is one of the
century's outstanding crime novels.

He dismisses the whole "mystery" genre as trash, on the
simple ground that it is badly written. His aesthetic standpoint
can be put in one line: style and structure are the essence of a
book, and great ideas are hogwash. That will hold good for
Mansfield Park, for *Swann's Way*, for *Ulysses:* those are not
crime novels. When we reach his beloved *Madame Bovary* we
will say Stop: he is so dazzled by its virtues that he does not see

the wood for the trees. The matter (we shall see why this word is insufficient) and the theme of the crime novel are death and destruction—the ruin of the body and the distortion of the soul. Vital: central to our existence. VN's dogma is rooted only in aesthetics. Were it true, then *Rosenkavalier* would be as great a work of art as is *Fidelio*. And it isn't. The "mystery" genre is trash because badly written; agreed. But also because it trivialises a noble theme. I think I can make a shrewdish guess why this should be so, but our concern for the moment is the prism.

Every schoolchild knows that the prism splits light into the spectrum; that this band of colour ranges from the hot reds and yellows to the cold blues and greens; that pictorially the artist keys a composition to the cool or the warm. In music or literature we make play with vague terms such as *classical* and *romantic,* and we can see and hear in terms of colour, and we can say that the cool end is more intellectual and the warm more emotional, that Mozart is cool and Verdi hot. The spirit will of course range along the entire spectrum, which is in fact circular. Childishly obvious?—but this helps get rid of all the muddle that surrounds, preposterously, the whole area of crime fiction. Dickens was a hotly emotional writer, and this much influenced his Russian admirers. Flaubert was a notably cool writer, which in turn formed a whole generation of followers, perhaps most remarkably Conrad. We the readers (Nabokov says, how justly, we do not read—we re-read) tend temperamentally to love more the one or the other, which is why—myself—I prefer Stendhal to Flaubert (and why many people cannot abide Dickens). Tastes also are subject to historical variance: we live in a time where the generalized preference is for the cool and the dry. Mozart was not highly thought of in the early years of this century, at a time when Bruno

Walter's conducting, now heard as hopelessly ove
was greatly admired and Toscanini's Verdi the
musical art.

This is all germane to our view of crime fiction
Shakespeare, the emotional white heat of *Othello*
was straight up Verdi's street. Now we like the co
atmosphere of *Hamlet* better and the cool comedie
The public will rush to a *Così* and would pooh-
Freischütz. The Wolf's Glen in the second act is
fustian: a great mistake.

Scratch a major artist and you will find a
Scratch Nabokov's *Lolita;* Lionel Trilling rightly sa
book about love. The themes of suffering, remor
tion, atonement have far more weight than any p
of this gross elderly man's forcing of a fourteen-ye
Humbert's love for Dolores Haze is not ignoble.
intent is deepened by the satirical scenes, which a
marvellously comic: the imagined assassination o
"our Glass Lake," the actual murder of the Fie
rable art). This is sophisticated high comedy, but
analogous situation in *Rosenkavalier,* recalling tha
eighteen is rather more innocent and considerabl
experienced than Dolores Haze at fourteen. The
renouncement of her young lover is great art and
but there is no crime involved because there is n
ciple at stake. Since her marriage is merely a co
adultery is technical: her cherishing of the
Humbert's her worries about education and pr
ing) is upper-class good manners. She renounce
selfishness and vanity. (Is it so? Sung by Lotte
showed true nobility, and this nobility Humbert

The cool end of the spectrum may be typed by

mental donnée of the detective story is that the deaths are no better than crossword clues.

The answer I believe to be quite straightforward. Materialist philosophy, and a refusal to believe in afterlife, has made its greatest strides in this century. Foreseeably, we have a great and paralysing fear of death, because all the goodies are here and now, and death will take them away. How pathetic (but solemnly heard, humourlessly clutched at) the pronouncements of scientific Bumbledom that we now all live ten years longer. Fictional death then becomes rather popular: it happens to people who never had any life.

Othello can then be lived with: weird things go on in Cyprus, but they're all wogs, anyhow. Verdi could write a pretty choon. As for *Wozzeck,* if it ever happened (much better if it had not happened at all), then to European Neurotics. The awakening, in England, has been extremely painful and is still a subject for disbelief. What? Our police force, like everything of ours the Envy of all Lesser Breeds, is corrupt, sadistic, fakes evidence? We won't believe it: "crime" is something light from the public library . . . No, no, that won't do; life is too serious as well as too short to leave to literary editors.

Major writers are few, and we also need the minor ones. Not those who in Nabokov's words "do not bother reinventing the world," squeeze the best they can out of a given order, and ornament the commonplace. These we read, when we have nothing better, but these we do not re-read. We need those defined by John Updike in his introduction to the lectures. "He asked, then, of his own art and the art of others a something extra—a flourish of mimetic magic or deceptive doubleness—that was supernatural and surreal...." I have myself preferred the word *metaphysical.* Our professor speaks of that telltale tingle in the spine. He does not mean the Fat Boy who said, "I wants to make your flesh creep," but the excitement of perceiving something new and something true, which we call creation. I have suggested—and I maintain—that the writers of prose fiction have in crime themes found the straightest way.

My editor (such things are much within the provenance of good editors) found that this statement "asked specific questions," to which I must try to give brief answers.

Do people write crime novels in an effort to make order of chaos? If today's generalized belief that life stops with death is chaotic—yes, certainly.

I should call such a belief supernatural, pusillanimous, swollen by vanity. I would not be far from calling it illiterate. All art cries out the reality of metaphysics. Every thinking scientist (their vanity is excusable, since they are thought of and treated as today's priests) will accept that there is no such thing as an exact science. Without metaphysics, there isn't any physics . . .

Does the crime "reported" (that word has to go in quotes) reflect the realities of society?

Reflect? Yes, since these realities are reported in the press and infect the writer. The smallest gleam of light will enliven the prism.

Are they stronger when entirely the creations of a specific imagination? Certainly, even if it be a trick question. Nabokov asked his students to notice how Flaubert, supposedly the most naturalistic of writers, took enormous liberties with factual probabilities.

Does the availability of crime novels create an atmosphere in which "crime" in actual terms becomes "normal"?

Aha! There are indeed great numbers of bad crime writers: one must look at the how and the why. To heighten their effects, they rely upon titillation of mankind's ignoble instincts: voyeuristic, and sadistic. This compulsion will make ordinary, decent men and women travel fifty miles to be present at the scene of some blood-boltered road accident reported on the radio. They will see a knot of official cars and some flashing blue lights. Make no bones about it: this is enough to get some dicks up, to moisten some vaginas. A fact of existence may be, and often is, ignoble. Following a rape or a murder (in metaphysics the despoliation of body or of spirit will be the same) there will be a rash or outbreak of denunciation, often self-denunciation. As the poet (a formidable metaphysician) W. H. Auden wrote:

> *When the green field comes off like a lid*
> *Exposing what was much better hid. . . .*

But one must not make the common mistake of confusing taste with morals. The vulgar crime story may be execrable pornography, but the prohibition of drugs, whores, or dirty movies would be the Volstead Act all over again, and the censorship of books is a virulent symptom of fascism.

We approach the year 2000. Among yesterday's smaller news items it was stated that Professor Stephen Hawking's book *A Brief History of Time* had established a Guinness record for sales longevity: if so a wry little fact, since notoriously it is unread and even less understood. A cheerful sign still? A pointer, perhaps, that a world brought despairingly low by materialism could still find remedy in metaphysical thought? I am reminded of Thornton Wilder's play of the forties, *The Skin of Our Teeth:* "One more squeak like that and where shall we be?" Mr. Antrobus placed his faith in books, and I recall the beautifully written scene of "nine o'clock I used to call Spinoza."

I have done likewise, and my nine o'clock I have called

Stendhal. My belief is simple. With this key Shakespeare un-locked the heart, and these are some of the books which hold keys to survival into a century that promises to be very dodgy indeed. The great crime fiction of the nineteenth century is not necessarily a better key to an understanding of metaphysics than Professor Hawking, but I should suggest more available. For a guide towards entry into the twenty-first century I offer the closing lines of *Little Dorrit,* which I have cited elsewhere in this book.

Grandfontaine, France

Criminal Convictions

❧ Crime and Metaphysics

METAPHYSICS IS INDEFINABLE as a fact of existence, and the word itself defies definition, but can be illustrated. Any art will do, though poetry and theatre together form the most potent, perhaps, of ingredients. The texture of material life is dense, but sometimes thinner and more transparent, so that at times one can hold up a candle and something of this transparency will be perceived. Ingmar Bergman was sensitive to this truth. I think of the moment in *Fanny and Alexander,* a work full of such metaphysical glimpses, in which the old actor grimed and costumed as Shakespeare's Fool, sings the quatrain "When that I was and a little tiny boy"—the lighted candle had been placed on his head and many people wondered why.

Words are poor things and the prose writer has a hard time of it. Language is imprecise and vocabulary inadequate, and those are formidable obstacles to lucid expression or enlightened discussion; today both the spoken and written word are thrown about like garbage. Ease and rapidity of communication have broadened no path towards wisdom: the glut of verbiage makes for mental indigestion, intellectual diarrhoea. The politician obscures his meaning so that he can deny a pronouncement become inexpedient. The businessman employs bad faith to evade a charge of fraudulent description, while the lawyer is praised, and paid, for expertise in verbal chicanery and learned confusions. The scientist claims that numbers are precise, while words are not, takes pride in illiteracy and the invention of meaningless neologisms. The little boy who saw that the emperor had nothing on, and created a scandal by saying so, would now have his simplicity bewildered by breakfast-food advertisements. Science has become schizophrenic, while art has turned into public relations. A professor must pretend ignorance of a commonplace Greek word, historia, meaning enquiry, and be bullied into speaking of "her story" . . .

In this world the metaphysical realities are swept under the carpet. The disturbed mind has ado to struggle with material untruths; if it cannot trust a literal statement how shall it cope with a spiritual content? Paranoia, the mind beside itself, resolves metaphysics, the reality behind matter, into the claim that only matter is real; all else will be inventions of pseudo-Oriental gurus whose abuse of human credulity can be measured in terms of a Swiss bank account. As Dr. Trelawny (genial invention of the novelist Anthony Powell) is fond of saying: "The Vision of Visions heals the Blindness of Sight."

A physicist derived the not-word quark from Lewis Carroll's not-thing, the snark; at least, this illustrates nescience. In trouble with an indescribable which has neither weight nor dimension, he shows some metaphysical awareness and speaks of its flavours. Crime offers the same difficulty: what is it exactly? In a world where both "good" and "evil" have become quarks, the Flavour of the Month applies. Language, now the toy of journalists or Presidents, was in the sixteenth and seventeenth centuries a splendid and precise tool, as witness Milton or Cranmer. Thus Lord Justice Coke, defining the crime of murder: "The unlawful killing by a person of sound mind of a reasonable creature, under the King's Peace, with malice afore-thought, express or implied." A noble sentence, clear as the note of the tenor bell. Nothing indeed written by subsequent legalists is anything but obfuscation.

Nonetheless we are troubled by this definition. Surely the King's Peace precludes riot, unrest, war, and do we not live in a chronic state of all three? What is a sound mind? The English legal definition of insanity, still called the McNaghten Rules after a celebrated decision of 1843 based upon the personal prejudices of Queen Victoria, is a notorious farce. The accused in the Moor Murders of 1965 were tried with no reference whatever to their real state of mind. Other countries, while guffawing heartily at Brit Wiglomeration, have not in fact done all that much better. There has been a notable acceleration in meaningless murders, often multiple and without profit or advantage to the author. Neither legal nor medical mind has coped to anyone's satisfaction. Metaphysics will not explain, nor give comfortingly moral certainties. The candle, upon the head of the Fool, will still lighten our darkness.

As with politics, opinion about crime has a left and a right wing. It is by some people held that crime is no more than the result of bad upbringing and worse environment and could be curable or at least diminishable by the betterment of both; a starry-eyed viewpoint. More and better psychologists, as a remedy against holocausts, is a belief sustained only by psychologists. Others maintain that if only the laws given by God to Moses were properly applied instead of being progressively diluted by weak-kneed lawgivers, everything would be tickety-boo. Punishment is the thing. But strictly for other people (it is arguable that all extremists suffer from their lack of humour). And as with most areas of opinion the populace will be found huddled in the middle. Huddle rhymes with muddle: they prefer not to think at all because when they do—as when something nasty has been seen in the woodshed—the populace becomes vengeful and bloodthirsty. The honest are ashamed of this, recognising that fear leads always to violence.

Texts of attractive simplicity and reassuring certainty can be found to support whatever shade of opinion, from "Judge not, that ye be not judged" to "An eye for an eye." Vengeance is mine, saith the Lord: it isn't quite clear whether right now or in some unspecified hinterland carved above church doors by medieval stonecutters in which we all hastily assume sheep's clothing while all too recognisably goat-footed. Disquieting, very, and I have seen a Belgian Benedictine, a man with such respect for life he would not squash a slug, tell an Irish peasant audience: "You'll all go to 'Ell." Poor theology.

Founded upon fear and irresponsibility, these slogans won't get us far. When being fearless we have generally been doped by some artificial stimulus: Honour, or the Fatherland; the quick prospect of Paradise and a flow of adrenaline; the fear of being cowardly; the need to know whether one can still spit. Most of us were brave last Thursday, not quite sure whether we will still be so tomorrow. If Death is a big adventure, one would prefer to stay at home and read about it. As any nurse can tell you, some people take themselves in hand, and others do not. Metaphysically speaking, the avoidance of responsibility is a mortal disease.

This is present in early childhood, as when we say it wasn't I who broke the window, but to learn responsibility is the initiation into adulthood. Avoidance takes sophisticated forms, such as the Good of the State; governments set an extremely bad example, and the collective irresponsibility of administrative bodies is notorious: there is always someone else to blame, and nowadays a computer. It is thus always present in crowds. It feeds holocausts: but we've got to get rid of the Jews, "everyone agrees." It is fed by facile jargon: "I must have been insane." This is at the root of most crime. "Listen—you know—I was just so frustrated." It is nourished by the pleasure principle, linked in turn to the fear of death: if I don't grab the goodies now, there won't be any later on. Whatever is nice; sex, or pie, or scratching where it tickles, is good for me even if it's bad for everyone else.

Irresponsibility, this ugly and clumsy word, translates into a characteristic modern attitude, tolerance towards oneself while being intolerant to all else. If thus I am drunk at the wheel of a car and kill someone (this particular lethal weapon is within the reach of all) I will react by suing the liquor store and the garage attendant: they didn't warn me. While I'm at it, I'll sue my doctor for malpractise in failing to tell me it might happen, my insurance company for not seeing that I'm the victim, and the police, who weren't watching the road properly.

This doctrine feeds my vanity. An administration can be bribed, for these people are small fry, thus poor, thus to be despised. Higher up?—everyone needs a favour. A court?—I'll get a good lawyer. Dear, but money's no problem—join a syndicate. Bills come in?—sue the syndicate. I feel a bit low? Phone Mrs. Jones, tell her to come over.

We have tried to build safeguards against this, with systems of ethics to control it, but as well defy gravity; we do try to rise but predominantly we sink. For vanity, in the denial of responsibility, will go some way to assuage fear. For a little while. My vanity will lead me to kill a lot of people if this will make my fear easier to bear. It will lead me to think myself intelligent. My sanity will be squabbled over by lawyer, doctors, who think themselves bright but are all morons.

If only it were that simple, but metaphysics has other traps for us. A glimpse can be had in the lives of ordinary men, promoted to power; Philip II perhaps, or Hitler, who lived lives of blameless austerity and took their responsibilities seriously. Philip went to Mass daily, when it wasn't twice, and insisted on seeing and annotating every state paper. Hitler ate the simplest vegetarian food and had the utmost distrust of corruption. Admirable men. Lacking humour, perhaps. After falling from power Mrs. Thatcher used the expression "Funny old world." People are so ungrateful.

We have only one sound key to metaphysical truth. We are aware of the barrier. We realise that the gateway is the moment we fear and attempt, ludicrously, to deny. We try to hold a candle, looking for places where the wall of incomprehension may appear thinner and more permeable. Traditionally we have sought in the areas of experience called mystic, in philosophic adumbrations of emotional kind, and on theological premises. One can find much that is admirable, obscured by the bulging sackload of oddities and the mystifications of the charlatan: it is a discouraging search. Art is nearer to hand, perhaps more reliable; the data are more convincing: any major picture gallery offers striking examples. We begin by calling them magical. But there is no sleight of hand, no illusion. We can go back again and again. This method has the advantage over similar experiences in nature, when one inclines to believe that exaltation or fatigue has played an over-large role in the quality of the experience. I have neither training nor aptitude in music, but surely the aural sense is as trustworthy as the visual? One must cite subjective examples, which those of greater knowledge and skill will examine. Thus, "the three Fs," suggested Erich Kleiber (like his son arguably the finest conductor of his generation): *Freischütz, Figaro,* and *Fidelio.* I will agree; others will find others. For I belong to an unhappy race, those who cannot grasp mathematics, a grave impoverishment. I know that numbers have metaphysical properties, observed also in the intervals of music, the proportions of architecture, painters' subjects which exert particular fascination: a tree, a naked body. I reach out numbly for words to express that which I apprehend. I mumble, like the physicist with the flavours of the particle, about my taste. Words are so impoverished.

But they are all I have: the bent I discovered in my childhood was literary. The reasons are genetic and environmental: I grew up with books, without a piano. A child directs the force of imagination—unimaginably powerful and vivid—towards the means of control it finds, subconsciously, the most malleable.

Early—I was eight in the year of his death—I fell under the influence of Rudyard Kipling, and count it a great good fortune. An admirable master, who wrote a beautiful supple English; in his early days an unequalled storyteller and in his mature years a writer who has haunted my whole life, my every day. He wrote towards the end a memoir called *Something of Myself* conveying, notoriously, almost nothing of himself, but this withdrawn and secretive man does speak of his encounters with the metaphysical world. Now and then, he says, his pen fell into the grip of something stronger than himself. It came most strongly—the barrier was at its thinnest—around three or four in the morning, and most often when a southwest wind was blowing. It was my first lesson in metaphysics. It is real and it can be detected in his printed words. He called it the Daemon. There is no comment to make: he accepted it.

Later it would strike me that this could happen on any level, even that of simple entertainment. To his friend Rider Haggard he said, "You did not write that, you know; something wrote it for you." The artist who, occasionally, experiences this influence notices that it takes an emotional channel rather than those of reason and logic, and that it is followed by a wrenching sense of deprivation. Peter Abelard, the greatly gifted, sees it as God, which in his century is natural. Very likely it is so.

But if a novelist, and I was thirty-three before this was at all clearly apparent to me, then why a crime novelist? It seemed to me an accident that my first entertainments fell into this category. Or so my first publisher, the shrewd Victor Gollancz, assured me. It had been no conscious choice of my own. If so it seemed fortunate, for in 1960 this was a tired and laboured genre; there was a premium on freshness, and room for a lightweight talent to amuse. To possess it is a great gift.

Yet for some years I felt a sort of rage. Why was this genre treated as escapist fiction on the most trivial level, good only for reading on train journeys, or to rest the superior mind from intellectual labours of more exalted nature? This was certainly nonsense. True, the average English or American detective story had no more merit and deserved no better fate than the *Times* crossword, and the gangster tales belonged in the "twopenny blood" comics I had read when a small boy. Could one not do better? And if one did, what was needed to avoid permanent consignment to the dustbin? Still—one could earn a living. And perhaps, after long years of arduous apprenticeship, one might learn something. Be that good or bad work, might it eventually arrive at an avoidance of mediocrity? One of the great difficulties in art is that the mediocre appeals to those of mediocre mind. Of whom there are many.

To mature thought, crime is a phenomenon of significance as much metaphysical as material. Inherent is a destruction of mind more frequent than that of body. A murder arouses our attention: loss of life reminds us of our fear of death. It is irrevocable; there is no way back. But it is trivial by comparison with the crimes against the spirit, which may strike in childhood and leave a long trail through the years of ruin and suffering, which can infect generations still unborn, which can create syndromes of deficient immunity in ways more deadly than a slipshod blood transfusion or the wish for sexual pleasure. Crime, factor ever present in social behaviour, is of unforeseeable weight and consequence. Indeed, the element of sexual satisfaction in criminal projects is ill-understood still, and ill-described. To take an example come only recently to light, it is said that a Lord Chief Justice had to change his trousers after passing a death sentence. Some would throw doubt upon this. I find no difficulty at all in believing it.

In prose fiction, crime is the preeminent and often predominant theme. With few exceptions—one thinks of Jane Austen—the novelists of the haute époque through the nineteenth and well into the twentieth century found their central source and impetus in the romantic, naturalist, and psychological treatment of the theme. I have attempted to discuss some of these in detail, in these essays, and it should be clear that the choices made depend only upon personal taste: one could have found as much to say—but with less enjoyment—about Madame Bovary or Melville, Dostoyevsky or Henry James. The selection of Stendhal, Dickens, and Conrad is arbitrary; they have given me so much, and still do.

If art be a doorway towards the metaphysical world, crime is a window upon it and sheds light? I distrust metaphors. Conrad spoke of the shadow line to describe the moment of apprehending this invisible domain. He found keys in work and in the sea; these went together, since life at sea meant unremitting toil, and fatigue increased perception. His overriding theme is that of responsibility—in the first instance that of mate or captain answerable for the safety of the ship: everyone aboard it; everything in it; whatever chance meeting or occurrence. To reach out for, to accept the "I answer for this, I and no other"—that makes the man; nor is he truly man until he has brought his acceptance of both worlds to the limit of his capacity. It can be too much for him; it will kill Martin Decoud and be the ultimate ruin of Nostromo. His perception can never be entire, and that is man's privilege as well as his tragedy. Kipling made the same point. So did Professor Tolkien: those elves and hobbits are not really for children.

Crime may be no more than a momentary failure (I find the long-drawn romanticised melodrama of *Lord Jim* exceedingly tedious). The "crime of passion" has found a sudden weakness in our elaborate armour of self-regard. Our condemnation will go, rightly, to a deliberate avoidance of faith and betrayal of trust. Mr. Verloc's crime is not the placing of a bomb, nor even blowing up poor Stevie. It is against Winnie.

The novelist is handicapped by the feebleness, the imprecision of his words, his chosen medium. He envies the painter, who curses the unreliability of chemicals, or the musician, whose violins are never truly in tune. Who has the closer, the more direct access to the human heart? Each can do what the other cannot. The artist, to the world an eccentric and quite pleasantly barmy, is—also in general—personally violent, unpredictable and unreliable; in human terms often a mental defective. The converse holds good, and the mentally handicapped are often remarkable artists; their metaphysical alertness and awareness are greater than ours. The fact has led many to speculate upon the role played by the jester in medieval courts—as it were, a metaphysical antidote to autocracy and crime. Or the dwarfs in *Las Meninas*—a summit, surely, in pictorial art? There was a congress (Figeac, France, July 1991) of the mentally handicapped, who there displayed their arts. Peter Brook, the man of the theatre, was struck by the splendour of these talents. And "yes," remarked a doctor who works with them (quoted by *Libération* of Saturday, July 20), "one has a metaphysical envy of these people." The French word *envie* contains both envy and desire.

We do not know at what moment the man or woman who commits a crime of violence can be held responsible. An *Observer* report of the same date upon the syndrome of the battered wife and the legal doctrine of provocation is before me as I write. We know less still, in a world where irresponsibility can be so generously rewarded with wealth and fame. A court, in Europe, can be turned upon a hairsbreadth. Release? Imprisonment? A psychiatric ward? And which will engender the most suffering?

What is the artist's given work? To be an honest witness to his times, to hold up mirrors? He cannot be truly objective; always he will be the prisoner of thought and of senses, of emotion shaped by birth, by environment, by experience. His duty, and his answerability, will be to increase awareness: among the normal of this world; those who ignore or deny; those whose sensitivities have not been awakened.

Crime is the pathology of the human condition, the moment after, it may be, a long drawn-out disturbance or perversion, at which the delicate balance of metabolism—decidedly, this prefix pursues one—tilts into morbidity.

As with all pathological conditions it is sad, sordid, smells bad. Woe then to the pathologist who should lack self-awareness, humour, and humility.

What is one then? The doctor? Or the mental defective?

✤

❧ Stendhal

I N STYLE AND method Stendhal is so startlingly modern. In the first years of the nineteenth century the novel was what it says, something quite new. Prose was stately, elaborate; this writer's informal, conversational voice comes as a surprise. He is the first "crime" novelist because he was the first to see crime in terms of ordinary human emotions. Crime is a predominant force in society because the State, itself, is in its nature and concept a great evil. He writes, as others do, about God and Government, about Love, and Honour, and Duty, and the conflicts these high themes awake in the human heart, but his manner seems a century ahead of his times, and his declared ambition—to keep one reader still in 1930—is strikingly farsighted. His enemies are cant, hypocrisy, and, in his favourite word, baseness, by which he understands the use of power towards self-serving and ignoble ends. Topical in 1930, he will be just as much so in 2030—if anybody then still knows how to read.

It was in part his talent, for no more vivid pen ever set prose upon paper. His life was also remarkable. He was French but as much as Goethe he was a European, an internationalist, and even today, in France a unique phenomenon. He was the son of a petty magnate in Grenoble, in that materialist, litigious, hard-headed Dauphiné captured from the Habsburgs and still very Spanish in character. All his life he would see Italy as the antithesis of all he detested in France, and today he is the standard-bearer of all who are born into La Grande Nation and in revolt against the stifling mediocrity and small mean-mindedness of French chauvinism. The Revolution took place during his childhood. School drenched him with the new ideas, with the physical and political sciences; he loved mathematics. He also detested his father and adored his mother; these powerful distortions and ferments would greatly fuel an incandescent writer.

The influence of a powerful protector brought him as a student to Paris; got him a commission in a cavalry regiment. He appeared in uniform, in Napoleon's new viceroyalty of Italy, decided that arms was not his profession, but ever thereafter would see Milan as his home and Italian civilisation as his patrimony. There followed some obscure and fairly ignoble years of commercial traffickings, until Count Daru found him a post in the military supply branch of the imperial administration. Here he rose to positions of importance. He made the campaign of 1809 in Germany, and of 1812 in Russia. "Stendhal" is a little town in eastern Europe, an intersection of supply lines. He was at Moscow, and thereafter abandoned Napoleon's service, but these experiences were to give him the finest evocation of the futilities of warfare we have in literature, a twenty-page *Gone with the Wind* sharper than anything in Tolstoy or Thackeray.

After the Restoration he angled, often ignominiously, for a civil service post, and was named as consul in Trieste, but the Austrian government refused him. He was too widely known by then for liberal and thus "dangerous" sentiments. He got, eventually, the second-rate sinecure as consul at Civitavecchia, which he held for the rest of his days without ever taking these duties seriously; it gave him, at least, security, leisure, some comfort: what a writer needs. He pottered to and fro in what we now call the Midi, admired and enjoyed England, became a good authority upon the arts, and wrote tremendously, but in desultory and disjointed fashion. There is much about painters and musicians; there are travel diaries and biographies and a very notable autobiography; there are essays, a scattering of tales and novellas, but only three full-length novels, and one of those remains unfinished. He is judged, nowadays, upon the other two and the astonishing *Vie de Henri Brûlard.*

In his time he was much admired (he got a flaming review from Balzac) but he has fallen overmuch into the hands of academics: this prefatory note may not come amiss. It was the time of Byron (whom he met and admired); his heroes get into Byronic situations and live them in the High Romantic manner. Ambition, love, passion, death are the mileposts of his fiction. More easily forgotten is his veneration for Scott; decidedly, these young men are generous and not calculating (a sure sign of baseness), as they would be in France. His own young men model themselves upon Napoleon, vow themselves to great things and believe in action. They are like the writer too, prolific and scattery. Fabrice, when set upon the road to a good career, embarks upon a foolish and frivolous love affair, a Stendhalian way of behaving. In polite company where a good impression was needful Stendhal would become bored, get drunk, and make outrageous jokes. Fearful remorse next morning. He was far too intelligent for his own good.

Le Rouge et le Noir, the book for which he is best known, is very much a young man's work, while *La Chartreuse de Parme* is mature; less violent, and less angry. But one must speak of both. This brief word allows no space for *Lucien Leuwen,* fascinating though it is, nor for the brilliant but wayward shorter fiction.

The Red and the Black: the title stands for Julien Sorel's two aborted careers in the Church and the Army, which alone could propel a young man of peasant origin into the upper classes. The book is a ruthless analysis of a ruthless young man who will stop at nothing on his road to power, wealth, and social position, and who will end very fittingly on the scaffold. He will act out his own death with Byronic splendour. Julien is atrocious but has striking qualities. The book has great impetus; there are few dull passages. It is filled with bitter sarcasms and a ferocious raillery of all that the writer most detests: what we now call the Right Wing. Monarchy, Church, and Aristocracy are allies in reaction and corruption, interested only in preserving privilege; but most of all he hates the greed, the jobbery, the hypocrisy of the bourgeoisie. The Abbé Raillane, false priest and police spy, is detestable, but still worse is Monsieur Valenod, the source of whose wealth is the municipal orphanage. About them all, he is wonderfully funny.

For the romantic young idealist baseness begins with physical or moral cowardice and will encompass all crooked, sly, and ungenerous behaviour. Self-abasement is unforgivable; Julien is the most Jansenist of Lucifers and must rise to every challenge he sets himself. This is marvellously detailed in the two, justly famous, high points of the book, the chapters called "Ten o'clock at night" and "One o'clock in the morning." The first is pure comedy; the timid and impoverished young tutor of Madame de Rênal's children has to kiss her innocent and virtuous hand before the clock strikes, whether or not she has him sacked, slaps his face, tells Monsieur de Rênal, or all three. It will lead in fact to his death. He does not know that, but would still do so if he did. The second and grander set piece is as remorseless, a blacker and higher comedy: he must climb the gardener's ladder, from the courtyard overlooked by every eye in a grand Parisian town house, to reach the window of Mathilde's bedroom. He is quite convinced that it is a pretext to have him assassinated for this insolent attempt upon her very upper-class virtue—but he must still do it. Mathilde will understand it, and will see him as her destined husband, but he does not know that. It will bring about the fulfilment of his every ambition, but we—we know that he is doomed, from that first timorous step outside his village rusticity. Byronism cannot be pushed to more ironic a conclusion.

The writer has two lessons for today's crime writers. There are no sex scenes; Mathilde simply tells Julien that he is going to pass the night with her. And there is no gallows scene; merely one splendid terse sentence: "Everything happened with simplicity, correctly, and upon his side without any affectation." That, and rightly, is very famous. The book is a masterwork, and yet I dislike the chill detachment of Stendhal's approach. Mathilde de la Mole is a magnificent heroine, her beauty, pride, and vanity admirably drawn. She is perhaps best seen in the light of that later, and sentimental romanticism in which the century would so indulge. Thus d'Artagnan sets out from his village in the same spirit as Julien, and will happily seduce Madame Bonacieux as well as Kitty and Milady in pursuit of ambition, but it will not occur to him to try his charms on Anne of Austria, for he sentimentalises her queenly condition. Another Dumas hero, and Mathilde's ancestor, does indeed get into bed with a queen, and loses his head for it. The romantic legend which neither writer could resist is that Marguerite de Navarre claimed her lover's head from the executioner. Mathilde, who wears black upon the anniversary, will do the same; Stendhal has achieved a fine irony but does not attempt a metaphysical dimension. The "greatness of soul" he speaks of is lacking, and this is an impoverishment. Fabrice, in the later book, will achieve this, and through renunciation rather than death. But every young man should fall in love with Mathilde (a ravishing tall blonde), and should feel himself "absolute for death." It is a young man's book.

In *La Chartreuse* a wiser, warmer—and thereby also funnier—Stendhal is at work. A fine writer is often better thought of for the energetic insolence of early books; Dickens is a classic example and so is Kipling, and *Le Rouge* too is often placed above the later, riper but more demanding masterpiece.

The book begins on the same lines: Fabrice Valserra, disgusted with mediocrity and his odious papa, runs away to join Napoleon's army before Waterloo (described in an ironic set piece of exemplary skill and economy). But things are not quite the same; it is the writer's joke upon his earlier manner. Fabrice is also a younger son, humiliated and despised, but his father is not le Père Sorel, that acid portrait of the tough, sly *franc-comtois* peasant, but the Marchese del Dongo, and Stendhal's comment upon the "noble" family is to show him an abject figure terrified of giving offence to the Austrian occupiers; a grovelling collaborator as we would today call him.

The young man must be taken in hand, and his Aunt Gina though herself a penniless young widow makes a plan. His only chance of fortune will be in the Church, and once ordained he will be presented to a sinecure; Coadjutor in the mini-state of Parma, where Gina's grand new admirer is prime minister, with plenty of political pull. And indeed, the Bishop, kindly old man, takes a great fancy to his brilliant young assistant. But the great snag, as Fabrice is warned, is the Prince; worst possible of reactionary autocrats and surrounded by a clique of toadies hostile to the Minister, Count Mosca.

All this is hilariously funny; Stendhal gives full play to a riotous sense of humour. The great difference from the earlier work is that the comedy of situation is subtler and more delicate. New is that this entrancing farce, like Mozart's *Marriage of Figaro* will turn out to have metaphysical resonance.

At first all goes well, for Mosca, while thought deplorably liberal in outlook, is high in favour, and Gina is made Duchess de Sanseverina, for the Prince admires her greatly (to the disgust of the clerical party) and is indeed dying to get into bed with her. But beware; Fabrice is young and inexperienced, and may provide a banana skin on which the whole left-wing party might slip.

*

Le Rouge is set in France. In the Italy of Arrigo Beyle, Milanese material interests are not pursued with quite such single-minded and humourless purpose. The new book sparkles in contrast to the cold and caustic wit of the earlier; it is full of people who make jokes; there is a play of light and shade at odds with that grim gloom that lay upon Verrières and the Faubourg Saint-Germain.

Europe just after Napoleon's fall meant monarchy restored in a climate of brutal reaction, born of the terror inspired by a glimpse of republican ideals. "Liberal" thought would be repressed with severity; autocracy more absolute than ever made its authority felt in rigid regulation of society. Today we would call it Stalinist; it was then Austrian and embodied in the name of Metternich. They had been badly frightened by Napoleon, who was not content with kicking them out of Italy. He parked soldiers in imperial palaces, bedded an imperial daughter, treated the Emperor with impatient condescension, and worst of all (in the eyes of the virtuous) bustled both the Pope and the slowest, most sclerotic bureaucracy in Europe. There was a general feeling that God and Paperwork had not met with respect: this must be remedied. When the northern Italian provinces reverted to Austrian rule their hand was heavy. The scenery of *La Chartreuse* is that of a frontier, guarded along the imperial borders by a horde of excise men, police spies, informers, and passport officials. Beyond the frontier lay a patchwork of city-states much as they had been in medieval times, governed by autocrats whose authority was backed by fortresses, prisons, and a police as repressive as the Austrian and even closer by. Stendhal's Parma is the microcosm of that fascist state, a century later, which the "one reader in 1930" would recognise, complete in every ludicrous and atrocious detail. Hitler and Mussolini both would remind that reader of the Prince, Ranuce-Ernest IV (irresistible comic name).

*

Of course Fabrice slips: he has a little affair with a dancing girl. Her gigolo, attempting to bully this mild and timid young man, pulls a knife on him and gets spitted. It is plain self-defence—and exactly what the clerical group has been praying for. The Prince condemns him to death; in an uprush of sadism commutes this to perpetual imprisonment, at the prayer as he proclaims of Gina, said to have "cast herself at her sovereign's feet." She has in fact told him what he is and what she thinks of him: it is his extreme mortification which exacts vengeance. We must not worry overmuch; Gina will arrange for Fabrice to escape from the dreaded citadel of Parma, abetted by the governor's beautiful and virtuous daughter, which sounds like a lurch into sickly sentiment and—conspicuously—isn't.

So far, thus, a socio-political novel, but the crime themes will take prominence, developed with a vigorous comic irony rather than the bitter sarcasms of *Le Rouge.* These themes were a hundred years ahead of Stendhal's day and are topical now. The behaviour termed *criminal* and so defined by a penal code of law is to be seen in the light of personal responsibility accepted, or evaded. The State is a concept based upon the power principle, and a denial of responsibility. It is thus itself criminal. It exerts political and economic pressures, forcing wrongdoing upon the individual, while its own blacker evils are hidden under a veil of hypocrisy, whitewashed by propaganda, and when laid bare covered by the *raison d'etat,* a term stretched to enrobe the basest ignominy. This is no mere Nacht-und-Nebel ruling, but the bread and butter of our democracies. Character assassination and physical suppression are the common form of every government, and Stendhal's rule of responsibility is also Václav Havel's.

The second half of the book has been criticised for lacking the pace of the first. It is true that there is less action: it is a profound study of the meanings of crime, of guilt and sin, a questioning of Christian ethics and political science, such as we will find in the Russian novelists fifty years later.

We are wary today of the word *crime* because it has been emptied of content. The penal code, those pedantic and antiquated injunctions, is no more than a field for the chicaneries of expensive lawyers; a net to catch the very poor and the mentally deficient. Even the flippant old saw "not to get caught" can be disregarded, since it ensures publicity. The grounds upon which we now pursue and judge aberrant behaviour are uncertain when all can be explained, excused, and at the worst amnestied, when forgetfulness has taken the place of forgiveness. To feel guilt has become the grosser crime, to be ashamed of and to be combatted. We do not like to pause, to ask whether we are guilty, and what of. Crime has always been a label which the rich are fond of sticking on the poor, a bourgeois concept. Offences against property were always more severely judged than those against the person, but the shoplifter is a thief, where the accountant had a little moment of weakness. In northern Europe crime is a Protestant, Puritan idea, meaningless in the south: we do not understand the Mafia because the poor take altogether a different view of crime or of guilt. Franco's police went about measuring the length of girls' skirts, while the Duchess of Medina Sidonia went to jail for being a Red. The phrase "I shit on God," in the United States a horrifying blasphemy, is among the milder of Catalan expletives; you would say it if you dropped the spanner on your toe.

Henri Beyle is a child of the eighteenth century, with a sharp eye to the split between theocentric and anthropocentric ethics. Guilt is the binding thread of his narrative.

Fabrice has killed a ruffian in a brawl? As the Prince remarks petulantly, a gentleman does not do such things; he hires them done. But Fabrice feels guilt; of putting his friends into jeopardy, for they must take extreme risks to save him; of toying with a young woman, and trivialising her emotions. Gina feels acute guilt; her caprice may bring about her nephew's disgrace and death. Mosca feels guilt; he has been cowardly, truckling to the ignoble ploys of his Prince. Clelia feels overwhelmed with guilt at falling in love with a man whom she has been trained to look upon as both priest and criminal. The Prince himself is guilt-laden in his vanity, fear, vulgarity, and meanness of mind.

One of Stendhal's great merits is his refusal to sentimentalise. There is nothing here in common with Hugo's *Misérables;*

that great showpiece and high-water mark of mid-century sentimentalism. Indeed, the famous dedication "To the happy few" makes clear that he will have no truck with romantic triumphs of justice over oppression. Marius will sail off into the sunset with his Cosette on his arm, but Fabrice over slow years will come to terms with himself as a responsible, adult man. It is a metaphysical solution. A redemption through religion? Only on the last page of the book will Fabrice enter the Charterhouse of Parma. Clelia, and their child, are both dead. Over tyranny there can be no triumph in a world from which justice is excluded, and only a happy few can accept that. Now nearly two centuries later, his tale has accumulated in power.

In passing, Gina has an excellent claim as the most enchanting female character in fiction. Some critics hold Clelia to be a flaw; one can't blame them—she is a young, romantic girl and the Duchess de Sanseverina is a full, mature woman. These critics are in love with her; so is everybody in the book; so am I; so are we all.

In one of the later scenes Fabrice is found on his knees in church, giving thanks to God for an escape from death. In an astonishingly modern comment Stendhal contrasts a freely given and unselfseeking penitence for wrongs done with those extracted confessions, so prominent a feature of Stalinist, today's Chinese show trials. He notes that within the conventions of the Church one did not confess sins, but asked the confessor for guidance as to which sins one should feel guilty of. Stalin invented nothing.

We need a historical perspective to *crime* and only fiction can really give it us. Reading this book one can often be reminded of the Crusade against the Commies which for fifty years has obsessed and perplexed the United States. To be told as we are now that the Kennedys frequented whores or that Cardinal Spellman fancied choirboys can be seen as a trivial commentary upon much greater crimes. Stendhal has said it all, perhaps long ago but not at all far away.

✤

❧ Charles Dickens

THE MAJOR fiction writers of the nineteenth century are all major crime writers, and where an exception occurs it will also be major. Jane Austen is exceptional in most of her ways. If we do not think of them as crime writers this is because nobody then had put *crime* into quotation marks. The world was a place of great excitement and overflowing with energy: new thoughts, discoveries, possibilities arrived practically every minute. Crime, like wearing clothes or going to the lavatory, was so constant and compelling a factor in society that no one dreamed of isolating it as a phenomenon. It was there, as sex was, or money, or bread and butter. One didn't talk about it much: one tried to avoid the more unpleasant penal consequences, such as getting hung or flogged or sent to Devil's Island. In the first quarter of the century one could very well get clapped into prison for petty debt and stay there too, quite possibly until one died there. It might well strike one then. What is this crime then? Is it the same as sin? Is it just being unlucky? If you were young, extremely sensitive and enormously gifted as was Charles Dickens, then yes, you started thinking about it. You started writing about it the very moment you got a pad and pencil as a little jump-the-gutter reporter, and all those years later when you were rich and famous and dying, it was still on your mind.

I am writing about Dickens because I love him; and about Stendhal for the same reason; and Joseph Conrad; and also because these three between them occupy, and populate, and illustrate the whole of the century. If I were an expert, which of course I am not, upon Balzac or Flaubert, Trollope or Thackeray—or the Russians—or Henry James—my arguments would be much the same. There is no denying that Dickens is the most obvious choice, especially for an English boy whose father read aloud great masses of him, with immense relish.

This is so rich a mine that all too easily I would lose my way. What could I say that has not been said already? Treasures of thought and reams of prose have gone into enquiring how John Dickens, the respectable civil servant, came to go to jail, and how this trauma in his son's childhood came to create a psychological pressure so intense that it never left him—the century's best-selling fiction writer and still the Child of the Marshalsea.

I do not much like the early work. I read it, again and again, enjoying it as though for the first time. The difference is that now I know exactly where to skip. This is of no interest and to put it on paper would be as boring as it is self-indulgent. Suppose I do say that I like *Barnaby Rudge* and find it shockingly underestimated or that I can't even bring myself to open the *Old Curiosity Shop* and find *Chuzzlewit* deathly boring; others have said exactly the opposite and their opinions are as good as mine. Nearly everyone seems to go on finding *Copperfield* the grand summit of Dickens' oeuvre; I think it tosh, and lamentable. Who cares? "Oh, Tilda, I do so palpitate"—no, I don't, and that's my bad luck.

So that in passing I have to condense my opinion into a brief sentence, if any of what follows is to make sense. I find all the early and even middle Dickens not much more than prentice work and practise ground for the real achievement, the four immense late novels: *Bleak House, Dorrit, Great Expectations* (to my mind the real summit), and that very odd book *Our Mutual Friend,* which is so abruptly very bad, and still so astonishingly good. "The coat of arms of the Squeerses is tore"— yes—and the sun is gone down into the ocean wave. But what an afterglow still remains in the sky.

Briefly then: everything before this contains great splendours. But it is not just crude, or violent, or melodramatic, or sentimental—it is first and foremost unready. My contention is that only with *Bleak House* does Dickens reach true maturity as artist.

I should wish, momentarily, to suspend age and experience; to come to this book with the freshness of a student of nineteen, who knows Dickens only from the few purple passages found in school texts—Mrs. Gamp, I suppose, and the murder of Nancy, or Paul Dombey's death. Perhaps it would be better to have missed them; they are no preparation for the immense, thick, confused sprawl of the Victorian canvas. "Nine hundred and ninety pages, have I got to read all this?"

It is well arguable that at least half is marginal decoration, barely tangential to development, a self-indulgent froth of comic character "over-egging the pudding." Esther's narrative is likely to strike the student as dull (exceedingly) and mawkish (atrociously). It was a bold technical experiment thus to alternate first- and third-person narration; ultimately a success only if Esther's dread goodness has not driven us out of our wits. It is with rereading, and the Dickens student must learn to speed-read, and to skip with a free conscience, that the enormous cast illuminates instead of obscuring the theme. Impatience and irritation will be felt: the book will seem greatly overwritten.

Even that magnificent and famous bravura opening? Will today's harsh and impatient student mutter "Bombast"? I find it hard to judge. Not only had I known the book from childhood, but just after the war I saw the actor Emlyn Williams read it as a theatrical evening. A fine performance. But the audience certainly knew the book, as I did; they came for the illusion that this was Dickens himself reading. The actor had made up to resemble the writer, and was using his reading desk. He took the whole at a clipping pace and every inessential had been of necessity sheared away: he had to . . . The point is that this cutting made for a fine, taut crime story, and an effective piece of theatre, while missing the essential of Dickens. I think one must demand patience and sensitivity of my student, who will then reap a great reward.

Much will be found awful. For Mr. Bucket's forefinger or Snagsby's little woman, George's simple-minded bluffness and the sentimentalising of Jo; these are written so black, so heavily underscored that one mutters and shuffles with embarrassment. How then does it come about, the miracle?

For first reading suggests that here again are all the vices of early Dickens; that this is yet another of those complicated and unconvincing plots, dragged into resolution by a row of ridiculous, melodramatic bombshells. We are to be bludgeoned into submission. Hortense is stock cardboard, and French to make it worse; she's Temperamental, you see. And is not Lady Dedlock yet another of those tiresome fallen women who Victorians like to bawl and sob over? No greater bore can be imagined than the women in *Copperfield* and is this, then, going to be the same? We will mumble angrily that this is absurd. This woman, plainly of strong character, would never have allowed the odious lawyer to blackmail her as he does. She would realise that he'd never dare tell her husband. Nor would she have allowed a clown like Guppy in her house; she'd have had him ejected by the footman.

But this is not the way to read a book of metaphysical weight and intent. As well complain that Leonora's disguise as Fidelio is not convincing. In all good crime fiction, realism is of little consequence. It does not bother us that there was never a private detective like Marlowe, nor a commissaire of police like Maigret. Only when character is false to metaphysical truth does it fail. Before jeering at the story of Lady Dedlock we must take another look.

We are at the height, here, of the romantic era. The famous rhetorical denunciation of Equity seems akin, at first, to Hugo's splendid but sentimental diatribes, but it is no mere rant.

Years have passed since Stendhal's denunciation of a criminal aristocracy. The revolution of 1848 brought about the reign of bourgeois monarchies, and real power had passed to financiers and to lawyers. Sir Leicester Dedlock's position in society (a Tory landowner, able to manipulate elections) is doomed as surely as his wife's. Mr. Tulkinghorn knows this, and sniggers at it, and he makes an efficient villain for a simple crime narrative. But the real criminals are to be found within the fabric of bourgeois society and they are those very respectable gentlemen, Conversation Kenge and Mr. Vholes, treated by Dickens just this side of satire.

He had also to obey the conventions of Victorian moralising to sell copies. Esther will have a sunset-lit future, full of pious good works, on the arm of Mr. Woodcourt. Her mother, the fallen woman, must die on the street, of neglected pneumonia on top of exposure and fatigue. We respect her all the more. Stendhal, who himself died on the street, had once remarked that it was no disgrace when not done on purpose.

Lady Dedlock has done it on purpose. Was she wrong?

The force of these sentimentalities about doomed-fallen-women is best perceived when we compare our own, today, which are the diametric opposite. Any writer in the 1990's who dared to suggest that sex and cornflakes were not the twin pillars of society would be howled offstage. The woman today who keeps her knickers on is as sure of contumely as she of a hundred years ago who got hers pulled down. The subject was the great obsession of evangelical protestantism as of today's pleasure-principle: there are two sides to the penny, but it is the same sentimental penny.

We must peel off these facile attitudes; we will understand Lady Dedlock better. Given, we would say, her undoubted strength of character, she would have told Tulkinghorn to publish and be damned, if he could find the courage: Sir Leicester had power still enough to have ruined him. Guppy she would have kicked out of the house; the snufflings of Chadbands disregarded. A tattle of disgruntled servants, on a par with the spite of the dismissed Hortense. Why this surrender, one cries, why this absurd flight?

The answer I believe is not resignation but renunciation. She accepts death in defence of honour: not her own, which to her has ceased to have importance, but that of those she holds dear. Her husband, foremost; her daughter; the father of the child she has thought dead. Are we to think of her as a romantic idiot? It is significant that Sir Leicester's character is drawn to a symmetrical pattern. Before her flight he is no more than a dinosaur; reactionary, cretinous. After, he is physically paralysed but heroic, and rightly seen to be so.

Since the Jellybys, Turveydrops, et al., are numerous, appear irrelevant, and their irritatingly ludicrous names lessen their impact, a modern reader can easily lose sight of the reality, that here is a strong moral pivot, far-reaching, of metaphysical weight. The loose structure so thickly upholstered with farce is likely to swamp the student in its immense profusion of detail, and Krook's symbolic death (corruption ends by destroying itself and the "Lord Chancellor's" one-and-ninepenny gin finds a sardonic echo in Mr. Tulkinghorn's bottle of vintage port) becomes merely another melodramatic incident. One is carried along by the tide of superabundant energy but the trees conceal the wood. We must not be duped: the author is feeling his way towards broad and great themes.

For sheer enjoyment the book gains from rereading. Stendhal's ferocious portrait of autocracy as a state in itself and by definition corrupt is embodied in a handful of vivid comic characters. It is the classical method of a big Velazquez, grandly composed and pulled together with sweeping strokes of great force and precision. Dickens' pointillist method is to build up slowly in thousands of little dabs of light and colour. The design of a tremendous picture becomes apparent behind this gradual accumulation of momentum, as with a huge Seurat, but one must stand right back, give it all time, allow it to sink in. Stendhal is economical with his gloriously laughable big comic characters; the effect is the greater when they are used sparingly: we think of Fabrice's appalling father, or the Fiscal Rassi. Dickens, irrepressibly diffuse, scatters dozens, as was his nonchalant habit. The reader's hand itches for secateurs to prune this exuberant tree: has creativity become an indulgence?

But where to cut? Surely one would want to keep Mr. Chadband's discourse upon Terewth; does he not point the way straight to Elmer Gantry and all of today's American evangelists? We can surely do without Boythorn and Jarndyce. George and Bucket, are a nuisance; overdrawn, unnecessarily obtuse. Why do we need Mr. Bayham Badger or Matthew Bagnet, Little Swills, the Turveydrops, or Charley? Do they not risk muddying, diminishing the texture? The answer is that if we are to possess a major painter we must also put up with his foibles, however tiresome. To dismiss Dickens for facility and vulgarity is to abolish Picasso, Titian, or Bernini.

The hand is by no means always crude or heavy. Wonderful drawings abound, expressed in brilliant ellipse; Mrs. Pardiggle's skirt, or Mrs. Jellyby's stay-laces. Chesney Wold, Sir Leicester's grand country house, is coarsely painted; the Ghost's Walk is a bore as well as lumpish gothic; but the writing can come suddenly and marvellously to life in Volumnia's pearls or the debile cousin. "Far better hang wrong fler than no fler" (sentiments to be heard today in any overblown Cotswold mansion). Fine craftsmanship can be found on almost any page; witness Kenge beating time to his own voice, or Mr. Vholes' impaired digestion (due to the three daughters in Taunton).

The focus can at times be blurred. Skimpole at first appears as quite extraneous, an excrescence upon the book but forgivable and entertaining, a delightful caricature and really great fun. A superficial view, defended by as good a critic as Osbert Sitwell. And Skimpole is totally vile. The portrait of the false artist is startlingly modern. We must realise that this total irresponsibility is the most fertile ground in which crime breeds. It is a sketch for the more complex and more sinister portrait of Gowan in *Dorrit*. The point is that in *Bleak House* Dickens is still feeling around the beginnings of his major crime theme. The two books will be joined by a third. This theme, that of the corruption and eventual destruction of the entire structure of bourgeois Victorian society, will work out in richer and more complex patterns than in *War and Peace*. It will be at even greater length: it will have taken four big books. It will not, thus, have the unity of Tolstoy's broad-striding narrative. Has it the greater impact? That is very debatable, since we read Tolstoy's novel in the light of the Revolution in Russia, whereas we have still had no great dramatic culmination of the sort. It is along the way that we notice how closely Mrs. Thatcher's opinions echo those of Mrs. Jellyby.

Tulkinghorn is finely done. The slow screw, rustily corroding all that it touches, is the portrait of so many lawyers today, politically pertinent in the United States and increasingly so throughout Western Europe. He loves only power: that is his only real interest. He has no pleasures beyond his bottle of port. He has no family, no sex, no human relationship. His rusty black clothes and unassuming demeanour are a pretence that he has no vanities: he is vanity personified, the classical, the consummate criminal. Nor is he overwritten. His sadism, towards Lady Dedlock, towards Hortense, towards any woman, is perfectly in key with his humble, subtle contempt for Sir Leicester; his crude bullying of George with his sniggering hold over Guppy. Vholes is a brilliant variation upon the concept of respectable evil, but the drawing is a little too heavy.

Guppy to my mind is Dickens at his happiest; nobody has better seen the shabby-genteel, social-climbing clerk. It is broad comedy but full and rich. The mooning after Esther, the pompous jargon of "us lawyers"—but the lights and shades are more delicate than they first appear. His generous patronage of Tony Jobling, while being more subtly patronised by the appalling Bart Smallweed is among the best things in the book, for there is pathos in it, as there is in his absurd efforts to extricate himself from his imagined entanglement with Esther. He feels responsibility, which is more than Skimpole ever will.

The Smallweed family seem at first pure farce such as the

early Dickens excelled at; an outrageous invention out of sheer high spirits such as Bob Sawyer or the Kenwigs family? One is not then happy at their link with Tulkinghorn, who is not in the least funny; this jars. But this is not the schoolboy farce of Buzfuz, any more than Chadband resembles the Reverend Mr. Stiggins: this is the mature artist. The Smallweeds carry with them that touch of pure evil that no one in the book will escape. The entire legal profession is here utterly corrupt. It will take some few more years, and Mr. Jaggers, before the balance is restored; we will have come a long way from Dodson and Fogg. The Smallweeds are appallingly, frighteningly funny: evil often is.

One touches here the area of metaphysics, without which no serious art exists, nor serious discussion of it. That will come later, I hope, in this book.

For the metaphysical dimension exists in *Bleak House,* and strongly. Everyone, did I say, even remotely touched by the corruption of Equity, is ruined? But not, as Dickens makes it quite plain, Miss Flite. She is preserved from destruction by her madness, but it is a metaphysical madness, of the strongest significance.

She is generally dismissed as a fantasy arabesque such as Dickens is always fond of displaying, like Jenny Wren, or for that matter Lady Tippins, but she is a genuine metaphysical character, and we shall meet more of them in the later, profounder genius of an extraordinary writer. She is mad? Saner by far than the Chancellor: does not her litter of "documents" make more sense than those blue bags stuffed with chicanery like so many sausages? Foolish?—she has far more acuity than Conversation Kenge "with his documents." She confers estates, and is not "Accept my blessing, Gridley" richer, and more moving, than any estate that could be restored to the Man from Shropshire? Is not her kindness to the Wards in Chancery a better protection, and her advice more sound, than that of their virtuous and wealthy guardian? Her birds, when freed, will be unable to protect themselves and will be killed by the wild birds. Knowing this, she frees them. She is, at last, the only figure in the book to escape futility; herself and that other futile, noble figure—Sir Leicester Dedlock.

For Dickens is growing, as he never grew before, and there is no ending to *Bleak House*. To be sure, he gives us the conventional happy-ever-after conclusion; as George Orwell has remarked, nothing left for them but to stuff down enormous quantities of food and produce immense numbers of virtuous and well-behaved children. This is only the nod towards the Victorian proprieties. Dickens is launched upon his great, his real theme, and nothing now can stop him. Everything unresolved in his mind will surge forward anew, afresh, in a further leap of that splendid energy, splashing into the racing pages of *Little Dorrit*.

Little Dorrit is a poor title, both feeble and sentimental, and it is often a bad book; bits of it are so very bad that one has much ado to shake off the shadows thrown by some of Dickens' worst writing upon a great deal of his best. It soars still, an enormous symphonic work, grandly designed and executed, and it occupies the central position in his achievement; the essential bridge between the bitter sarcasms of *Bleak House* and the fuller gentler ironies of *Great Expectations*.

The cruder material symbolism of *Bleak House* is contained in the famous twin images of the fog and the mud. The sky is always the greasy soup tureen that would so appal the young Kipling in 1890. Is there a fire somewhere? asks Esther. Dear me no, miss, replies Guppy, greatly pleased with himself and his city. One will meet him there today, conceited in his finery and just as knowing about restaurants, or sharp practice. This, miss, is a London particular. Even I can remember these; there can be hardly anyone to recall the mud, diluted into a ghastly soup by the thin greasy rain in which Lady Dedlock dies: a mix of soup and trampled horseshit.

Nowadays, London is covered in the thinner if scarcely less horrible oil of diesel exhaust, and the sky is perturbed by the lacquers with which Mr. Guppy sprays his hair, but at least the air is clear of the roily billow of coal smoke and so too is it in *Little Dorrit*. The reader who overcame the oppressions, the toils and glooms, of the earlier work will, I should think, be captivated by the tremendous narrative energy and carried onward to the major masterwork. *Dorrit* is less asphyxiating in both setting and impact.

One reason for this is that Dickens detested the provincial, jingoist England (even today so entrenched); loved France and Italy, set a large section of his new book under lighter, airier skies. He saw, too, his theme more clearly, with the metaphysical eye of his total maturity and a new, far-reaching profundity. This is the book which Shaw said made him a socialist: the comment holds something of Shaw's silliness but holds like many of his sayings enough truth and sharpness of perception to make one stop and think.

It is a strange, at times bewildering, book of enormous audacity, holding some major successes and a few startling failures. The technical daring and psychological insights are radical, but there are still alarming recessions into the ranting manner of the crude, early melodramas. The writing has not the clarity and calm with which Dickens will at last satisfy his reader.

The sky has cleared more than a little and Amy, sitting on

the church steps as she waits for dawn and for the turnkey to open the gate of the Marshalsea, watches the moon and a racing cloudwrack: there is a world, then, beyond this squalid street and Maggy's shopping bag, and a power able to break the bars across her spirit. The wind will drop, and the great cloudscape in which Mr. Dorrit builds his castle will allow rays of sun to fall slanting, at one moment to create an unparalleled metaphysical image of a crown of thorns upon London.

The theme is still that of *Bleak House,* of a criminal society capable of redemption through a woman: read in tandem with the earlier book this theme is simplified and strengthened. In a double spiral narrative, itself grandly imagined, Arthur Clennam and the Dorrit family are both the victims of a great evil. This—alas—is to be resolved through a typically confusing and complex plot, which I for one have never wholly grasped nor had the patience to work out, so tortuous are its workings. If less flimsy and perfunctory a pivot than Lady Dedlock's baby—it is a deep-seated wrong that has induced Mrs. Clennam's traumatic paralysis—these laborious mechanisms through which Dickens seeks to hold together a vast and unwieldy narration have been the source of many grumbles. But we are rewarded by the splendour with which he unfolds a noble theme.

It will be as well if I try at once to excise the black blot that lies upon this book and goes far to ruin enjoyment. Dickens has felt himself in need of a villain-figure. The seeds of this personage are perfectly modern; that criminal vanity which takes the form of believing that the world owes one a living. When we first meet Rigaud he is on trial in Marseille, for beating up his wife; she died of it. A murder charge thus, and he risks the guillotine. A hostile crowd has gathered in and outside the courtroom, which he considers most unfair: he only corrected her a little, for failing to provide for his comforts, and the cow died to spite him. But he is confident of talking his way out of trouble; he always does . . . And he does, though Dickens does not tell us how—an initial flaw that widens until it splits the whole book.

This could have been a good concept, but unhappily, Dickens chose to make his villain French, in an ill-judged truckling to the habitual crude xenophobia of his public, and to give him physical adjuncts that are horror-movie clichés: a hook nose and sinister eyebrows, a greedy way of eating, coarsely underlined, a big black Dracula cloak. He says things like "By Blue," and calls people his "Little Cabbage." It is inconceivable how Dickens, who loved and understood France, could have been so silly as to allow this cheap propaganda to deface his canvas. Hortense could pass, as a device to thicken the shadows around Lady Dedlock; Madame Defarge belongs to one of the feeblest of all his fictions; but this demon-figure is here hideously out of key. Absurdly, ludicrously flitting in and out of the narrative, he will come close to wrecking it altogether. One tells himself, resignedly, that Dickens plots always are preposterous, but we had hoped for better this time. It is a relief to say now that in *Great Expectations* this flummery, as of Monks and the Jew tormenting little Oliver, will have disappeared.

Rigaud once exorcised we can breathe easier. There are more flaws, and Arthur Clennam is a basic failure. He is dogged by a miserable childhood and incapable of breaking out into the real world, but in fact he is a poor stick and it is difficult to feel the sympathy that the writer demands of us. It is arguable that technically he has to be dim, so that Amy's qualities (which are undeniably fine—she is an immense advance upon Esther) may shine the brighter. One still feels uneasy at

Arthur's incapacity to be anything but polite to everyone: he is likeable, but what a sad sack. Nor can one feel quite happy with the amalgam between an early nineteenth-century world in which imprisonment for petty debt was a commonplace, and this sophisticated late Victorian society in which Mr. Merdle's swindles could impose upon Bar and Bishop, and the Circumlocution Office reaches a pitch of ingenious prevarication quite in accordance with our experience today, but where the Marshalsea appears strangely anachronistic.

It is a wonder that he brought it off at all: admiration for the Inimitable is the more. Who else can be quite this bad while reaching so high?

The characterisation is of finer grain in *Bleak House,* and more profound. Perfunctory inventions have been suppressed, or turned into skilful abstractions like "Bar" or "Physician" (or the Barnacles, even if the schoolboy humour of "Tite" is deplorable). The world of petty gentility, such as Mr. Meagles or the appalling Casby, is less coarse in texture, and if the bourgeoisie (the Gowans or Mrs. Merdle) are treated with derision and plain hatred, the satiric line is more delicately drawn. Merdle himself is a caricature but is conveyed skilfully through the medium of his court. In the old comic-sketch style are Pancks and Mrs. Major. Remain two amazing metaphysical inventions, Miss Wade and Mr. F's Aunt, and that most delectable of Dickens' female portraits, Flora Finching.

One is not perhaps altogether convinced by Mrs. Clennam's household. It is finely imagined, vivid in the detail of the furniture, the meals (and metaphysically the marks in the dust). The trio with Flintwinch and Affery is satisfying, exciting—and tumbles alas in wreckage (like the house) with Rigaud's jarring entry. We are asked to cope with all the infernal nonsense of the box and the double, and we feel Dickens' own embarrass-

ment at the coy disguise of the "dreaming." "Such a dose?"—
as though we had to open our own mouth for Mrs. Squeers'
big spoonful of brimstone.

A parenthesis at this moment for a detail noticed elsewhere.
One of the minor characters, Daniel Doyce, is an engineer, a
specific English type of self-educated craftsman and highly
sympathetic for both Dickens and ourselves. The brief portrait
is encapsulated in the "plastic movement" of his thumb on his
spectacle case; a real and convincing touch. One of the Sherlock Holmes tales, admittedly among the feeblest, is entitled
"The Engineer's Thumb"; a little gothic horror story of small
interest. The point is made only to illustrate the gap between
two sorts of imagination. Doyce is alive and invades the reader
in one paragraph; Holmes' Mr. Somebody is a pretext for
some flimsy flesh-creeping. One wonders whether Mr. Conan
Doyle had been reading *Dorrit.*

Amy, who begins as an amalgam of pious Esther and moth-
erly Charley, grows; is a success, I believe, but only just. We
could have done without Maggy! Why does Dickens have to
thrust it down our throat? She is better when seen obliquely,
through her sister Fanny, a brilliant sketch, or her decrepit
uncle, or her absurd admirer Young John, a comic echo of
Guppy. But she hovers uneasily upon the verge of sentimentalism. The scene in which she stays out all night, and in which
fallen women flit about, leading us to expect the worst, is re-
deemed from mawkishness only by the fine lyricism of her eyes
raised to the London skyscape. Saintly she is, but it is real and
unforced, without sugary Estherdom. One loves her, and she
gains in stature as the book unfolds. In Italy she is shadowy,
rescued by the irony of Mrs. Major's complaint that Amy will
never learn to be a lady: she is closer to this ideal than ever
was poor Lady Dedlock. In the presence of Fanny (who is so

resolutely not a lady) Amy becomes alarmingly ethereal, and when she gets back, to sit sewing by Arthur's fevered bedside—Maggy hovering, inevitably—we accept her, but without real enthusiasm. Whatever his complex, ill-understood relations with the Hogarth girls, Dickens never does achieve a convincing portrait of a young woman. Bella Wilfer, who starts so well, suffers a collapse into baby-coyness as calamitous as anything in *Copperfield;* as we can see in *Great Expectations* his failure of nerve when faced with Estella is the massive flaw upon his finest book.

This is no place for discussion of his notorious hang-ups in all his relations with women: it is established that he had an immature love affair with the impossible "Dora," lost sight of her; in adult life discovered that she had become Flora. This mature portrait is not just a success: we delight in every breath she takes, and most when her breath smells of brandy. The statue-bride, so loving and so lovable as well as so funny, is a real woman, at her silliest full of hard common sense: she can even put some go into poor soppy Arthur. Her earthiness (Dickens stops just short of her telling us about her problems with constipation) galvanises the whole book, and an extraordinary instinct ensures that she shall always be attended by, arguably, the most astounding of his metaphysical inventions. Mr. F's Aunt (the sure touch, in this preposterous title) is an advance upon Miss Flite; her madness encompasses a much wider field than Chancery Lane. She strikes the most terror precisely at her most farcical: witness the scene, which no one but Dickens could have written, where she forces Arthur to eat the burnt toast crusts. "A proud stomach, this chap." One cannot blame poor Arthur for being so wet, but the judgement is prescient.

Miss Wade is a fine creation, before whom he stops short;

plainly paralysed by her suspected lesbianism he fritters her away in the course of the idiotic vaudeville concerning the box: a pity. Tattycoram, asphyxiated by her embarrassing comic name, suffers the same fate: woman and girl both have strong sexual attractions, and before anything of the sort Dickens instantly falls to pieces.

Flintwinch is a good invention, potentially a more subtle, minor-key Tulkinghorn. He is ruined by the absurdities of the "plot"; his ambiguities are keys that open doors leading nowhere, and it is fitting that in the end he should disappear. He is not altogether wasted: one has, rather, the impression that the writer has not thought him out, using him instead as a prop to an intrigue as decrepit and broken-backed as Mrs. Clennam's house. If Mr. Merdle had been developed as a character, Flintwinch would be seen as a Leporello to this Giovanni whose uncanny charms—we are never told how they operate—have bewitched the bourgeoisie into parting with huge sums. His lawyerly manner and assured behaviour show him to be more than the elderly clerk and confidential servant dressed a little less shabbily. One wonders what Balzac would have made of both Merdle and Flintwinch.

The crime theme is a widening of that in *Bleak House.* We are looking at the vulgar bourgeois world of the mid-nineteenth century, swollen with wealth and complacency, and how close it is to our own. Social reform is blocked by the Circumlocution Office. The poor are squeezed by the likes of Casby, slum landlords pretending to philanthropy. Small insecure businesses will be exploited by sharks in the Flintwinch mould, greatly developed from the crude caricature of Grandfather Smallweed but moneylender and blackmailer alike; only a lack of confidence and imagination stop him from rising to the level of Merdle, who thrives upon the arrogant smugness of the high bourgeoisie and even the ruling class: these themes are altogether modern and actual.

Here are four promising lines of development. We must add Gowan's ensnarement of the Meagles family; very well done, indeed quite terrifying. Skimpole was only a sketch of the false artist, but Gowan is a considerable portrait, and very sinister he is. Nor should one forget Fanny Dorrit's elaborate revenge upon Mr. Merdle; less well done, hastily assembled and then thrown away. Even for Dickens it is all much too much. He was accustomed to handling this vast wealth of thematic material with crude and unconvincing linkages depending upon his absurd "plot," which was supposed to twist the separate strands into a cable: they remain obstinately disjointed. He doesn't really bother! Such scenes as that of Mr. Merdle and Mrs. Gowan (two notable harpies) taking tea together are quite perfunctory and can perfectly well be skipped. He could always rely upon his marvellous comic invention to bridge an awkward gap. Thus Bleeding Heart Yard, where Pancks collects the rents for Casby, is linked to the Marshalsea by the glorious farce of Mrs. Plornish speaking Italian; only the Inimitable could get away with it.

For Dickens has concentrated much of his book upon the character of Mr. Dorrit, the amiable incompetent hammered by an interminable injustice into a mean-minded scrounger. The obsession is only too understandable; it was his own father. His parents battened for years upon their wealthy and famous son, and he tried to treat them with fairness and generosity. They would keep tapping: it left fearful scars. He had to write this obsession out of himself; he had tried, before, but Micawber is rubbish, while Mr. Dorrit is a considered and coherent portrait. But his bounding imagination had seized upon the notion of a Dorrit suddenly and unexpectedly restored to fame and fortune. This is done with grandeur. "The Marshal-sea becomes an Orphan" is a splendid set piece, but it is accomplished with dreadful hanky-panky (Pancks is well named) and lo—but oh dear, he has to plot. He must link Dorrit with the Clennams, he has Flora Finching on his mind, and back at the ranch, Mrs. Merdle . . . He is writing four books all at once, and they're all sliding about in the irresistible cataract of his imagination. Every day brought its new delicious fantasy and he cannot discipline nor organise the torrent. Nothing in *Bleak House* prepares us for this explosion, of all the fireworks set alight together. He is developing his new, magnificent, and immense crime theme, and by now it is clear in his mind, but he is still at sea in the fearful jumble of his early life and childhood. The result is a sort of godforsaken soap opera.

By summing every scrap he has of skill and charm, all his confidence tricks, by stretching credulity further than Mr. Merdle (with an equally captive audience), he pulls it off; just barely. The house tumbles down behind him, but unlike Rigaud, Dickens escapes. It is a great Huzarenstück. Paradoxically, while materially speaking he was destroying his own novel, he gives the reader a great wealth of metaphysical illumination. How does this happen? Very beautifully.

Dickens attempts his familiar, vulgar, sentimental resolution. Amy will marry Arthur, in the church where her birth was registered. And they're all there, sobbing away, heartful; Pancks of course and Doyce, Flora to be sure, Maggy naturally. The crude tidying has been done. Mr. Dorrit has died, mercifully protected by his castle. Mrs. Clennam is as good as dead (Flintwinch, roguishly, survives to be glimpsed, amusedly, in Rotterdam!). Merdle has killed himself and Rigaud is buried beneath the fallen house. But all the loose ends have been left. Gowan has already destroyed Pet, and will probably kill her, as Rigaud killed the dog. Those two pathetic figures, Miss Wade and Tattycoram, are back where they started. Fanny will destroy herself. All the sparks go whirling off into darkness, and what is left at the heart of the comet? Is it going to be just like the end of *Nickleby?* Amy and Arthur will have lots to eat, in between having lots and lots of children? Because there at the end is Amy safely married, with Arthur still clinging to her skirt (and Doyce with Pancks to ensure that they have a comfortable income).

The sneer is gratuitous. We may join with Mr. F's Aunt (she is there too) in saying, "Bring him forward, and I'll chuck him out of window."

But this book is about the world. When the dust has settled, many a more worthless man than Arthur has acquired self-respect through an upright, a vertical woman. The world is the Marshalsea. WE live our entire life in prison, as indeed Dickens did. And in the end it is possible to walk out of the prison, as Amy has. Carrying Arthur with her. It was Dickens' great and unfair grievance against Catherine Hogarth that she had not been able to release him from the writer's private hell. He made up for it in the last, fine, purple paragraph of *Dorrit.*

"The noisy and the eager, and the arrogant and the froward and the vain, fretted, and chafed, and made their usual uproar."

It is a fine cadence; the words will stay obstinately in the mind. Why did nobody write this upon a splendid, ornate, Victorian tombstone?

Agreement would be, surely, as close to universal now as it ever is that *Great Expectations* is the finest work of Dickens?—the most nobly ambitious in aim, the most impressive in execution? The opinions of critics smell, perhaps, mustily academic, for this has been a book much analysed by the learned, turning up with monotonous regularity as a text for university students. That is one sort of fame; another, perhaps more interesting, is that it delights the craftsman. No book of his has been more often adapted for other dramatic media; for radio and television, for the stage and the cinema. It is the most satisfying of his books. It reads aloud very well, and to reread in solitude, in the setting desired (for it is pleasant to picture bed, chocolates, cognac, candlelight—the flame just bent by the gusts of a southwesterly gale outside), what other earthly joys and comforts compare? Sex?—no, don't bother me just now.

How does this happen, since Dickens notoriously pleases, amuses, and especially nowadays drives one distracted? He may be the greatest English writer of prose fiction but he is also the most infuriating. Even this book contains a nigh-fatal flaw. But the writing has a tranquillity and a transparency he nowhere else achieved. There is no fussy crowd of minor figures, tiresome subplots, bravura tear-jerking, nor that restless manic quality.

The crime theme has grown to maturity. No longer those Manichaean embodiments of Good and Evil; neither an Esther nor a Tulkinghorn, neither Amy nor Rigaud. Compeyson, the "vile" figure, appears in a mere dozen pages, a necessary technical device, and Orlick is no more than a vicious lout for chiaroscuro purposes; we are as relieved to find no statues of golden goodness. Herbert Pocket is a human, an imperfect saint drawn with gentle ironic humour. Even Joe and Biddy escape that embarrassing saintliness; their simplicity is touching rather than mawkish. Theirs is not a priggish piety.

In the major figures Good and Evil are entwined with a subtlety unique in Dickens, and signalling his true maturity. Nowhere else will we find the like of Pip. He is vain, silly, selfish, and ungenerous, but he matures into a man. His destiny is throughout bound to that of Estella, who is likewise the fullest and most interesting by far of Dickens' heroines. And here at once one must tackle the great flaw. In the worst artistic fault of his career, at the behest of Lytton, who was being crassly sentimental, he agreed to the "happy ending," and it is simply awful. The artist has seen, quite clearly, that for Estella there is no redemption possible, but in this one brief access of false emotion he comes within a hairsbreadth of ruining his best book. Men, always intolerably self-indulgent on the subject of fallen women, may accept this new, sweet-and-sexy Estella; no woman can, does, or ever will.

We have to try and swallow it, to forgive and forget, because what comes before is so good. The girl was given love, as the motherless Esther/Amy was not—but what kind of love? We see her in childhood, already an accomplished little bitch: her satisfaction at watching Pip and Herbert fight is openly sexual, a sadism her own as well as Miss Havisham's. We have to be careful, for the sexual life of a Dickens heroine bristles with the unsaid, since officially she hasn't any: even in his last book Lizzie, and even Bella Wilfer, can—as in Noël Coward's variation upon Cole Porter—"only Just do it . . ." Estella's deliberate choice of the revolting Drummle tells us that she is wide awake, greedy, knows it, enjoys it. If sadist, then masochist too. Drummle will beat her up first and fuck her blind afterwards, and she's well aware of it. Officially, she is carrying out Miss Havisham's scheme, for which she has been trained, to lure men and to destroy them—and quite undoubtedly, Dickens' own personal self-pity is obscuring artistic endeavour. What on earth are we to make of Miss Ellen Ternan? The Victorian view of female sexual pleasure lasted into the 1950's. In Molly Keane's witty phrase, "It's a thing men do: you won't like it"—

Mummy's advice to the bride. We are supposed to believe that Ellen Ternan piously endured being taken to bed, while hating every minute of it. I am not convinced that it is mere male conceit that suggests to me she found herself liking it rather. It wasn't from poor, perpetually-impregnated Catherine Hogarth that Dickens got a notion like Estella. For Mr. Jaggers knows all about people like Drummle: he is both interested and amused. It is not just conventional Victorian prudery that forbids Dickens saying more. He was a hopelessly poor hand at love-making, could neither go back nor go on. Estella smoulders as though stifled. For Pip she is an unpleasant cockteaser. Today we can see Dickens as being rather lubricious at the idea of taking her knickers down, and it is for himself rather than for the pious public that he funks it.

Whereas Magwitch, the other great lever upon Pip's character, is an admirable portrait, and perfectly consistent. Society has made a criminal of him; it does not—cannot—occur to him that bringing Pip "into society" is morally more condemnable than any of his actions. A broad and bitter irony, most finely perceived. He can see the deed, enabled by the wealth amassed in Australia, only as suffering effaced and balance restored: himself as an Equity such as no Court of Chancery could conceive. The splendid ironic climax is that he affords the means of Pip's attaining manhood in exactly the opposite sense to that he so naïvely intends.

Pip's "growth" is beautifully written. This young layabout, guided by the kindliness of Wemmick, Herbert's gentle patience, Jagger's sardonic and unsentimental rule, is a poor stick, like Arthur Clennam, but grows, as Arthur does not. It will take the purity of Biddy as of Magwitch to rescue him from ignominy, but he can see, and take, steps toward self-realization. Dickens is remembering his own shame at his father's cadging and his mother's genteel pretensions. And mercifully there is no "plot" to lead him astray; we are spared the mysterious will and the putative parentage. To be sure, Estella is the child of Magwitch and the gypsy girl whom we do not glimpse beyond the strong scarred hands, but it is much more interesting that she should be the instrument of Miss Havisham's pathological distortions. The nearest we get to the melodramatic coincidence beloved of Victorian novelists is that Miss Havisham's betrayer and thus destroyer of Estella, as of Magwitch, is of course Compeyson. Satis House is a place of Freudian fogs and prisons, for Dickens' own marriage was in bad trouble, but the idea of the loveless union entered upon in a spirit of vengeance had been in his mind for some time; it had been Fanny Dorrit's. This theme now seen as modishly feminist is simply that of a writer trying to come to terms with his own failures, lightening his bad conscience towards the mother of his children. The obtuse husband and hopeless father is the better writer for it, for which we can be grateful.

The narrative simplicity strengthens and enlivens the book; there are no meandering nudges to remind us of what we already know, that Esther is Lady Dedlock's daughter and that the Clennams have wronged Dorrit. Instead the suspense element, which will play such a role in the coming hundred years, is marvellously written, indeed never better; the flight, pursuit, and capture of Magwitch holds a splendid excitement. It is inevitable, and no artificial climax crudely tacked on to support a sagging tale. The convict's return, spring of many a coarse melodrama, is totally free of sentimental outpourings.

That Dickens is at the summit of his power shows best, I believe, in the portrait of Jaggers; powerfully condensed and compressed, and the more impressive since both full length and many faceted. The stranger in the village inn, giving the startled rustics a sharp lesson in the rules of evidence and the folly of believing newspaper propaganda, is altogether new in Dickens (and as actual today as then). As Pip's guardian, so shrewd and cynical, full of sardonic humour while kind and even gentle—he is a strangely moving figure. What a step from the tiresome cardboard of Jarndyce, full of pernickety mannerisms, and the deader with every page. One can trace the ancestry. Here is a slice of Tulkinghorn, in the love of power, the coldness and cruelty—that nasty touch of sadism at the dinner party, towards Molly, whom we do not yet guess to be Estella's mother. In the calculating manipulations is a touch too of Flintwinch. But he is much bigger than either, has far more presence because far more humanity. Much in this man is bad, not to be washed off by that highly scented soap whose heavy symbolism is a reminder of the earlier, cruder Dickens. One feels an instinctive repulsion from this man who can so clearly see and enjoy the brutality of Drummle and Pip's humiliation, who knows that Estella's intellectual sadism is naïve and even innocent, who relishes the nasty fact that gross physical and sexual violence will meet its match in her hatred and contempt: it is a horrible train of thought. Dickens, rolling yet again with erected penis upon Catherine, humbly spreading her thighs to receive yet another unwanted baby, could still understand all this, but only with his pen in his hand could he command his own physical reactions.

Jaggers can command kindness, yes, and generosity. This man of law is above all acute in his understanding that justice is human and thus profoundly unjust, but it must prevail. He will fight for Magwitch, knowing it to be a lost cause, because he is a professional and turning lost causes into winners is his living. He can see that Pip is protected, by the innocence and goodness of Herbert Pocket, of Joe and of Biddy, but that Estella is irremediably doomed. It is this realisation that makes a non-sense of the sentimental ending. The public could not bear that Pip and Estella should not be reunited, but we must condemn Dickens, for Jaggers knew better. Does this man not fore-shadow that other dreadful "just" man, the marvellous lawyer, that wonderful defence of the hanging judge, Stevenson's *Weir of Hermiston*?

This new richness and duality, this extra dimension in Dick-ens, spreads delightfully, satisfyingly, into minor characters. There is much more to Wemmick than ever could have been to Pancks. One warms towards Wemmick, to the kindly simplic-ity of his delightful home life, balancing the cruel portrait of the professional clerk. Underpaid, overworked—what else could one expect from Jaggers—making good with a shrewd eye out for the portable property. He will overdo that one day, but he will still make an effort for poor silly Pip. With his un-derstanding of all things material, and incomprehension of a metaphysical element—(which he can still apprehend, while failing and fearing to face its consequences)—Wemmick would today be compiling statistics for the *Economist*. One finds there the same sense of the important that will always just be missed . . . Our own century is very solemn about the por-table property, and Business as a religion has much of the evangelical fervour of Dickens' day, much of the same sense of inflamed and woolly uplift—almost exactly the same total ab-sence of humour.

This fullness of dimension is at odds with the conventional view of Dickens. The hasty journalist, the bawling propagan-dist, the crude moralist—this is not their work. I think that today's young men and women are much repelled by the rabble-rouser, preaching the benefits of God and knitted woollies, and do not laugh raucously at the gallery of roguish comics in battered top hats.

My thesis is that progressively, in these three crime novels, the Elmer Gantry side of Dickens is cleansed. In *Great Expectations* we do not find the hustler, the shouter-down, the coarse prophet of uplift, the vitality expressed as vulgarity that causes the fastidious reader to recoil from the early work. Even his delight in farce is kept under control. Our instinct towards Mr. Wopsle is to feel sorry for him, to approve Pip and Herbert for feeling ashamed at laughing so hard, for trying hard to praise him, for buying him a much needed drink. And when the robbers break into Pumblechook's house, tie him up, slap his face, we meet that phrase which only Dickens could have written: "They stuffed his mouth with flowering annuals to perwent his crying out"—and we dissolve with laughter because it is after all a gentle punishment.

Nor is there that distressing lurch into sentimentalism; the unease which grips us at the death of Jo or Amy's scenes with Maggy hovers only at the tacked-on ending, when we are told to be sorry for Estella, and perhaps at Joe Gargery's sock-bed consolations. One does so wish he wouldn't say "Such Larks," but these are small blemishes.

Remains Miss Havisham, and what are we to make of her, nowadays? Not much perhaps until we accept that like Miss Flite or Mr. F's Aunt she is something more than a mad old lady. The parables of Satis House are crude—the stopped clocks, the cobweb-covered wedding cake—mere gothic flummery. One can't help thinking that the satin frock must be pretty greasy and smelly by now. One would have indeed no patience with this jiggery-pokery without the realisation that these adjuncts are like the skulls and hourglasses in Renaissance pictures and must be seen in the abstract. In the canvasses of the best painters can be seen unexplained metaphysical figures, personages given physical form.

Seen merely as the jilted bride avenging a treachery, using Estella as the instrument of despair and destruction, she is preposterous. As a surrealist portrait of women's condition she makes all too much sense. Long years of suffering and mutilation, the piled-up brooding over humiliation and frustration, the crippled crooked manoeuvres—these can be seen today and recognised anywhere. But from what unconscious did Dickens find the impulse to write these scenes? Miss Flite is only a shadow across his mind, a moth attracted by light, burned in the flame; flit, flutter. Miss Wade is scarcely more, wading in a symbolic river of bitterness whose currents entrap her. But Mr. F's Aunt—her name tells us that she is an abstraction more sinister than comic. She is never seen save in the company of kind, jolly, cosy Flora—who is always a bit pissed. We know that Flora had been the young girl, the writer's first love, for many years lost sight of, seen again in middle age in all her resplendent silliness. And she's Mrs. Nickleby—his mother—and isn't there something too of Catherine Hogarth, nipping at a concealed bottle to hide the pain of her sharp, sarcastic husband furious at her clumsiness and inability to keep things tidy? Who is this dreadful spirit, and who is the woman in the satin wedding dress? We remember that there were more Hogarth girls.

There is a fascinating detective story here and I lay no claim to knowledge: others have explored Dickens' emotional life. Miss Havisham has been beautiful, and Estella is a very pretty girl. The force of her sexual attraction is strongly suggested. I feel sure that he did sleep with Ellen Ternan. That they both felt a heavy burden of guilt in consequence. I know very little of her. I should suspect that she was one of those girls who were quite genuine in virtuous demeanour, who then discovered physical pleasure in sex, and became greatly fraught in consequence of conflicts. I find it remarkable that Jaggers takes such pains to obliterate all emotional involvement. His famous remark "I'll have no feelings here" is a lawyer's professionalism, and his knowledge of Estella's parentage is a lawyer's professional obligation to secrecy. But who knows what darkness there is in his own relationship with Estella's mother?

As remarkable is the collapse—rather than decline—of Dickens' next and last (completed) book, for really there is nothing to say about *Edwin Drood,* which has always struck me as being a trashy detective story whose sole interest is our curiosity as to how Dickens would resolve the dénouement.

We know that his physical health was by now in dramatic deterioration and that psychologically he was growing steadily more erratic. There are well-known markers, such as the railway crash at Staplehurst. One can still find it hard to accept that after this extraordinary trilogy, which to my view climbs towards a great summit of vision, clarity, control, he should lurch so abruptly into recession towards the excesses of his earlier manner. For concerning *Our Mutual Friend,* the first and continuing impression is that of confusion, beginning with the notorious non-sense of the title. I love this book, and I reread it with delight, but there is no denying that it's sad bosh. And it starts so well, too; the immense evocation of the river is fit to make Anna Livia Plurabelle huddle back into her shawl. This announces a great striding crime theme. The Bird of Prey, fishing for bodies upon the tides of the Thames, is a magnificent concept. Alas, he, and it, are to be struck down. The crime theme, lucid and splendid through the three major books, will end in a whimper; the soppy, glaringly melo, good-bad Manichaean shrieking of *A Tale of Two Cities*. The book announces a thematically majestic development, and is riddled with sentimental woodworm.

For the Boffins are quite as ridiculous as their name suggests; one cannot believe for a moment in the pretended villainies of the Golden Dustman: these are the cardboard contrivances of *Oliver Twist,* as is the absurd Rokesmith-Harmon double identity. One has high hopes of the two girls, Lizzie and delightful Bella Wilfer, only for both to disintegrate, the one into a pale palimpsest of Amy Dorrit and the other—alas—into coy whimsicality. The pattern repeats through all the over-many characters, compartmentalised in the old, tiresome fashion. The energy leaks away before they are fairly developed, into a tired and perfunctory hitching of each into their appropriate niche, the good to be rewarded with glutinous great lumps of turkish delight, the bad with vinegar and pepper. We are left with the two original references that the still-incomparable Dickens eye had lit upon, to be embellished by the still-incandescent imagination: Mr. Venus' shop, and Wegg reading aloud from the *Decline and Fall.* These stay in the mind and give abiding delight; rags and tatters from the Shaman's Robe.

It is all readable. The technical skills, which knew so well how to make the reader turn the page, are still nigh-intact. Here and there one will still meet the inimitable flash of phrase, the lightning-quick laugh. But the great crime theme is down, like Mr. Dorrit's cloud-castle, and all that remains is the after-dinner speaker who has gone on too long, who can still hold an indulgent audience that recalls his splendour, and whose loyalty will not let him down. We only pray that he will

not collapse before our eyes. Halfway through *Edwin Drood* it
would come. His death was mercifully sudden, and he would
never know how bad the book was. It is the dream of every
writer, and his final prayer. To go like that, with a script on the
board, the familiar joys and hopes scenting the air.

✣

❧ *Joseph Conrad*

I SUPPOSE THAT I may have been seven or eight years old when my father, who had won a modest crossword puzzle, spent the prize on a handsome if unwieldy set of the collective works of Joseph Conrad, done up in the solid lavish old manner by John Grant of Edinburgh and lacking only massive brass fittings, inch-thick mahogany, and a Master's Certificate. The sole point of this anecdote is that I came to this writer by chance and read him out of filial piety. Nowadays, Conrad is the prey of graduate students, enough of them to crew the entire Peninsula & Orient Line since inception: he was then very much an acquired and exotic taste. It is astounding to realise that *Chance* and *Victory* were in their day bestsellers, even if this recognition and accompanying wealth came at the end of the writer's life.

I am not ashamed to say that some of these portly volumes, in their maritime uniform of dark blue and gold somehow evoking Elder Brethren of Trinity House, remained read once only. Perhaps there are circumstances in which I should turn again to *Outcast* or *The Rescue,* but they would be slow boats to China: the prose is immeasurably (to borrow a Korzeniowsky adverb) stately.

A further group held appeal in immaturity, to a daydreamy

boy. I should not think that Rita de Lastaola could today conquer even a fifteen-year-old heart, but the bookshelves of my childhood were well stocked with Victorian worthies, Anthony Hope or Seton Merriman. The purpose of this essay, which admits frankly that I am no Conrad expert, is to single out two books from that impressive line. I must wonder, initially, why I have reread these two so often, love them with so faithful an attachment, admire them so; and claim them as formative influences—for to me they are among the finest of crime novels.

Both are central to Conrad's development. In the monstrous armada of Conrad criticism *The Secret Agent* has held an honourable place. *Nostromo,* as I believe, was underestimated and even neglected until fairly recently. I view it as the kingpost of his career, coming at the summit of energies and widest scope of vision. It is a splendid piece of architecture. It seems to me that here he said what was important to him better than elsewhere. Here we are free of the oppressive sultriness that for me weighs upon the Far Eastern tales, or those crankily Polish polemics that mar *Under Western Eyes:* the South American winds blow strongly and freely. *The Secret Agent* is a black and brilliant work, and marvellously funny—in chronology, the two belong together—but it is altogether smaller in scale and in impact, as though after *Nostromo* he needed a tight, domestic horizon.

But before any discussion of detail I must set down a conviction: that without these books which I treat lightly or even denigrate, even *Nostromo* would lose much of its message. One has to look all along the line, and the writer's career is seen to describe a great architectural curve. Works admitted to have little importance, even unashamed potboilers like *Mirror of the Sea,* have as I now see sunk deeply into my consciousness.

Books of great tedium—I cannot feel quite sure that I ever did manage to get to the end of *Lord Jim*—hold unmistakable treasures; perhaps no more than a phrase here or there of Conrad's quintessential thought, but this can still be enough to move a world. He is a serious thinker. Who are we? Where are we going, and to what purpose? What is our task? One cannot enter the most leaden of his narratives without the awareness that by sea and by land a mighty spirit is astir. He had no use at all for conventional religious observance but there is no better metaphysician in literature.

There are a hundred witnesses to the gibbering little man with the comic accent, forever borrowing money and complaining of the gout, and they all agree to his astonishing mind. Quarrelling with Ford Madox Hueffer, vituperating against "this damned jerry-built rabbithutch," or getting into a pet about Jessie's cauliflower cheese—she was not just an excellent cook, she has been woefully and wickedly underestimated—he is a very great writer indeed, and that in spite of writing thoroughly bad English. I have never been interested in the academic squabble about his thinking in French. I regard it as nonsense, since his French, while accurate and fluent, reads as rhetorically over-elaborate as his English: in the nineteenth century probably all upper-class Polish gentlemen sounded like this. Hueffer, who was equally fluent in French, speaks in gallicisms but doesn't sound in the least like this. I ought to know something of the subject, having frequently been cudgelled for writing gallicisms myself. Conrad's style, while technically very bad, is a wonderful vehicle for his thought. No doubt he would have been both as good and as bad a writer in French, but he chose to live in England and it is agreed that he gained much from his choice. Be they landowners or intellectuals, or as was frequent both, the whole European upper class of the nineteenth century had this immense and profound love of and respect for England. Sadly, it is not at all so today.

Conrad turned to crime themes much as Dickens did, in direct consequence of his need for a solid moral pivot to sustain serious fiction: it is clear as early as *The Nigger of the Narcissus;* it is manifest in *Lord Jim.* The jump from the pilgrim ship is no mere momentary lapse into irresponsibility; it is a great crime expiated over long years and paid at last in blood.

There are many signposts to the inception of *Nostromo.* He was free, or very nearly, of Hueffer. He would go on being strapped for money until *Chance,* but now he knew himself a good and a thoroughly professional writer, and with the support of Pinker (no writer has owed more to the gallantry and generosity of a literary agent) he could maintain his wife, and their small babies. Jessie's crippled knee, her intense dislike of Hueffer, the maddening running after the next cheque (for work promised much more than that performed): these were sore burdens, but there is a fine firmness of purpose and confidence to his approach towards the "big book." When it turns from a short story into an immense canvas he views it with serenity. Hueffer—of course—claimed to have a hand and more in the writing of *Nostromo*; I do not believe this for an instant. One can complain about *Jim* that the resolution and the atonement are so lengthy, betimes so tedious, but *Nostromo* for all its grand and far-reaching design will be far swifter, a great deal more exciting.

It is a benchmark in crime fiction, and seventy years on I think it a splendid pendant to *Chartreuse.* For Nostromo himself, the Italian peasant who is the true aristocrat of Sulaco, has much of Fabrice in him, and just as d'Artagnan is a sentimentalised Fabrice, so does Nostromo inherit the myth of Romance from Dumas' hero and explodes it: the lordly gallant who balances the pretty girl on his stirrup for her to cut his silver buttons is d'Artagnan still, mocking his own invincibility.

His title is, to be sure, ironic, invention of the "admirable Señor Mitchell," who is forever boasting of his Capataz' prodigious can-do. The little flick of humour (Mitchell's Italian is no better than his Spanish) grows to a greater irony as we realise that he can indeed perform every exploit demanded, truly is El Rey de Sulaco; and is prolonged into the tale of his inevitable corruption and end. This is done with great technical mastery. Conrad had been a clumsy and verbose narrator, and in the persona of Marlow would be so again; but this complex structure of flashback and flash-forward is handled with great assurance, each scene disclosing a further dimension of ironies blacker and more bitter.

For if Fabrice in the splendour of youth is still at the dawn of revolution an optimist, Conrad has seen too much of revolution, does not like it at all, and is intensely sceptical about the betterment of society. He has distanced his intrigue to an imaginary South American province but the futilities of Costaguana are those of a futile Europe: the Church that he detests is identical to that of Stendhal. There can be no heroes here, and the closest we will get is old Giorgio frying onions and muttering about Garibaldi, or Don Pepe quite ready to blow up the silver mine and himself with it, if that's what it takes to frustrate the "sanguinary macaques."

Neither of course are there real villains, beyond that oddly modern figure, the millionaire philanthropist in San Francisco (still today the bane of every country in the Americas). Naturally, blood-boltered ruffians abound and Conrad delights in making them farcical: all are ludicrous, all utterly imbecile. Serious characters, illustrating the whole political spectrum, are seen in the abstract, every one a prisoner of the silver (itself an abstraction). The only way to survive in a South American republic is to treat it as a colossal joke, as Decoud does, impelled to suicide, since he can no longer believe in himself. The parallel with Camus' *Peste* comes readily to mind.

Gallows humour is given free reign. Sotillo fails to notice the boat holding the silver, too busy torturing the little Jewish dealer who dies without the remotest notion of what is required of him, the rictus on his face parodying Conrad's ferocious laughter. Democratic institutions are ridiculed; talk of patriotism is windy rubbish; the delightful old diplomat is hustled off still begging for the survival of parliament (and how wry our own laughter, another century later). When peace and prosperity shall have been restored, the country is under clerical domination and the end will be worse than the beginning: the final irony is that dear old Mitchell, the pompous and self-satisfied narrator, hasn't understood a damned thing and admires it all intensely.

An astounding performance; Conrad's knowledge of the setting was limited to a glimpse in his seafaring years, a bit of superficial reading, some folklore picked up from Cunningham Grahame (contrary to gaucho machismo Nostromo rides a mare), but no fictional landscape is more skilfully articulated. The social and political climate is that of Stendhal's Parma; the criminal forces of vanity, fear, and vested interests are the same, but seventy years later he has the history of nineteenth-century colonialism to draw upon: Nostromo's destruction is that of a rich and innocent land, bled white to the chorus of pious talk about Progress. Holroyd the financier sees it all in the simplistic terms of Reagan-economics. The silver is wealth and the only problem is that it should be extracted efficiently. Charles Gould is the man for this; he will justify the investment.

Admirable choice, for Charles loves, belongs to this country; perfectly honest, excellent administrator, tenaciously English in strength of character, unmoved by bribe or threat. To secure efficiency he will bribe others, never too little or too much; it is not an unsympathetic portrait. Is Charles thus incorruptible? Only gradually will he realise that he too is corroded by his fixed ideas; the silver has taken possession of him; he is helpless. A fine portrait is completed by that of his wife: Doña Emilia is a kindly, generous woman who understands her own helplessness to alter or arrest the slide towards disaster. Madame de Sanseverina, an eighteenth-century woman, believed in action . . .

These central figures are shrewdly observed through the skilful use of minor characters. Thus Doctor Monygham has been tortured, and crippled, under a former dictator; surrendered to cynicism he accepts his impotence.

The major-key crime theme is most satisfyingly developed within the character of Nostromo himself. An uneducated immigrant docker, his strong personality has made him the chief of the Cargadores, and to lend his magical Capataz has become a mania of old Mitchell, for it tickles his innocent vanity to believe that "his" Nostromo can do anything. So he can; the courage and dash of a d'Artagnan saves the province from the putschist generals in Santa Marta. Only he can save the silver; so he does. Irony will dictate that only he knows the hiding place, and inexorable corruption will make him its slave. "I must grow rich very slowly." It will kill him in the last—merciful—irony: old Giorgio shoots him—as a southern peasant would even today—safeguarding against an imagined threat to his daughter's honour, refusing to believe that he has killed his "son."

It is well known that Costaguana is the foundation of Greeneland. It seems appropriate that England's finest writer of crime fiction in this century should have learned from the so un-English Pole rather than from Hardy, the great and so-English contemporary. The Dorset air is a little too damp and enervating? Through almost all of this century England has seemed wrapped in cotton wool. A sharper, more Berliner air is needed. This is the moment for a brief look at *The Secret Agent.*

Drained and exhausted, full of tetchy complaint about climates physical and mental, Conrad succeeded in raising the wind (the long-suffering Pinker!) for a winter in the south, unrolled his mat near Montpellier, and set to work upon the most narrowly English of his books. The reaction from Sulaco is so violent that Mr. Verloc hates to budge from suburban comforts on the smallest possible scale. Indolence is in his every—but the word *fibre* will not do, either physically or morally. "You are very corpulent," complains his paymaster at the Russian Embassy. His whole character is summed up in the famous phrase "an air of having wallowed all day upon an unmade bed." His moral cowardice is cut from the same cloth; he is too lazy to take any but the easiest way out of every difficulty. In that first splendidly comic page we know that the title itself is a typical Conrad irony, that Mr. Verloc, the most incompetent of spies, is about to become the most butter-fingered of terrorists. In fact the theme of espionage is peripheral to the book, for Conrad tells in a page or so what Mr. Le Carré takes a few hundred laborious pages to say; that spies have no real moral centre, do not even know which side they are on; their patriotism is as much a fake as the rest of them. The confusion they exist to create has eaten them from within until they are mere shells. They bore Conrad. The "robust anarchist" and the rest are mere caricatures. Mr. Verloc is given a vaguely "continental" background but all this is very perfunctory. What we have—it is another far-reaching irony—is a classical English detective story of the most cosy Clapham-omnibus type, with a murder, a Scotland Yard inspector, and a chain of deduction. It is amusing to speculate upon what a crime reviewer would make of this; one of those gentlemen specializing in facetious three-liners.

Everywhere in *Nostromo* is the sense of distance. By ship or by railway, on horse- or mule-back, even on foot across the Sierra, journeys are long and perilous. Himself distanced—from the south of France, London appears as far away as Santa Marta—Conrad reduces his whole book to a quiet, shabby little street; to that minute squalid shop where Mrs. Verloc sells contraceptives, surreptitious pornography under a counter of grimy sweets and yellowed stationery.

All that will count, at last, is that stuffy little kitchen reeking of cabbage and suet pudding, where Mrs. Verloc sews the label into the collar of Stevie's overcoat, so that if he gets lost he can be readily identified . . . And that terrible little dining room adjacent, the good furniture carefully polished, the sofa where Mr. Verloc likes to repose after a heavy meal, where feeling uxorious he will summon his spouse for some sticky lovemaking and where instead he will get the carving knife.

The story is so simple as to be told in a few lines. The Russian Embassy (already!) wants a terrorist act, and Mr. Verloc must carry this out; none of the anarchist group will stir a finger. Target is the Greenwich Observatory—"The blowing up of the first meridian is bound to raise a howl of execration." A poke, that, at familiar "British" complacencies. Verloc to be

sure won't do it. Winnie's little brother—pathetic, backward—is easily persuaded into the carrying and setting of the bomb, and of course poor Stevie drops it in the park and succeeds only in blowing up himself. Conrad takes much relish in the detection, characterising in marvellous and familiar phrases: the policeman given the unenviable job of collecting bits of Stevie pokes at them "as though with a view to an inexpensive dinner," and he has fun with a minister: "Their idea of secrecy over there is keeping the Home Secretary in the dark." Naturally, Stevie is known by the label on his collar, but before the police can pounce Mrs. Verloc will do justice herself upon that ignoble sneak. Distraught, she will confide in one of the feeble-minded anarchists, attempt a halfhearted escape by the Saint-Malo boat, and overcome by despair, throw herself overboard. As is quite obvious, the real interest of the book lies in the character and psychology of Winnie Verloc. Where did Conrad get that, and what so focused and concentrated his mind?

He knew very little about women—unsurprisingly; it is the case with most of his contemporaries. His background indeed ensured that he had known few women, and they had played no great role in his fiction; even in *Nostromo* Mrs. Gould and Antonia Avellanos are adequate portraits and no more. Suddenly, he himself was to claim that *The Secret Agent* was really Winnie Verloc's story. There is nothing especially complex or difficult about Winnie's psychology; startling only in that she is a woman of the people, a figure rare in the bourgeois fiction of the time. She perplexed, and much upset, the obtuse reviewers (a tribe that hasn't changed much).

I suppose it possible that nowadays the feminists will have set up an outcry about Jessie, but until quite recently the

lengthy and learned discussions about Conrad took no account of her existence. Everyone was much astonished at his sudden appearance with this plain, awkward, uneducated, and apparently unintelligent girl. She was by far the most important influence in his life and career. Her calm and common sense, her unflappability, her warmth, and her humour made her an instinctive choice for this so volatile man, so tense and so intense. This ever-faithful, ever-loyal, patiently mending and remaking Heimat was not just anchorage and harbourage. We read, and with astonishment, of Pinker's unfailing support. At the time of *The Secret Agent* Conrad was a thousand pounds in debt to Pinker; in those days a gigantic sum. One is thereby happy to think that with *Chance* and *Victory* the agent balanced his own accounts and gave his author a comfortable and unworried old age. Without Jessie he would have been a writer, of course—he already was, and what was in him had to come out—but I am perfectly sure that he never would have been what he became. Just as Hueffer's influence has been greatly overestimated (it was of course valuable in the crises of self-confidence), Jessie's has been ludicrously minimised.

I notice that from those impressive *Collected Works* of Conrad I picked out *Nostromo* and *The Secret Agent* rather as though I were being clever, and as though nobody else had done so. I chose them, to be sure, because they are my personal favourites and because (the argument is the same) they best illustrate Conrad's handling of crime themes, and they have much influenced my thinking on the subject. I had, though, forgotten that the same two titles had been singled out by Leavis in *The Great Tradition*. Whatever people say about Leavis now, he was a very good critic.

However, it is fair to say that I had carried those two books to my desert-island library long before reading Leavis, who moreover does not see them in the context of crime writing, the area in which for me they have been so central.

�֍

❧ Sir Arthur Conan Doyle

"LOOK ON MY works, you mighty, and despair"? No such notion would ever have entered Conan Doyle's head. True, two vast legs stand in the desert, and certainly they belong to Sherlock Holmes, but that is hardly Doyle's fault. He was a very decent man, would have found the idea preposterous; the response would be a loud guffaw.

One might think that only the French could lack humour to this extent. They are greatly given to deifying minor writers: elevated Poe to a place in the stars, and Agatha Christie; Doyle would complete a Blessed Trinity. But people from all over the world have expressed similar sentiments, out of all proportion. It is worth the trouble to wonder why.

He was a gifted, a splendid writer. And a good man, who went to bat for Oscar Slater (condemned on no good grounds and unjustly imprisoned for a great many years) and managed at last to free him. Doyle used his great reputation, and consequent wealth, in many good causes and if sometimes a bit dotty—keen on spiritualism and a number of Victorian hobby-horses of the sort—he was always on the side of honesty and generosity. He fought chicanery and the mean-minded: one feels gratitude. And Holmes is an extraordinary achievement. What figure, around the world, has so captured the popular imagination? In the remotest jungle the peasant brightens, sketches the pipe and the hat with hand movement: "Scher Lok Oms." The great Victorians, Gladstone or Livingstone, have not this fame. What is this secret? What magic? In England, the ultimate immortality is to have a pub named after one, but to be, worldwide, a household word? Somebody, with the difficult job of making cosy an airport restaurant in the Aleutian islands, will slap his forehead and mutter, "Eureka"; six weeks later the place is full of hats and pipes, the menu features Mrs. Hudson's scrambled eggs, and the chap reels off in pursuit of a socking bonus, beaming fatuously.

Why, finally, should I put in my pennyworth? The Holmes literature is already colossal, as large an industry very probably as in American universities was conjured out of James Joyce. Decidedly, this is rum. The Victorian adjective, like "capital" as in a rum do, a capital dinner, can help put one on the right path. The salient feature of this character is eccentricity and sheer originality: these were qualities much prized in Victorian England. Add the magnificent self-confidence abroad, the gigantic rudeness. "I engaged this room in 1886," shouts Mr. Chowdler in G.F. Bradby's "The Lanchester Tradition," expelling an intruder from a Swiss hotel, "and I intend to keep it." Well known is that Doyle when a medical student was struck by the personality of a professor who demonstrated the value of sharpened observation as an aid to clinical diagnosis: it became a student game. "Beyond the obvious conclusions that you are a bachelor, a solicitor, and a Freemason, I know nothing whatever about you." It grew, spontaneously. Doyle would add nearly as many phrases to the language as Kipling: the dog that did nothing in the night-time, the asking for an amnesty in that direction, the "eliminate the impossible and what remains?"—to this day the French will say "Elementary,

Watson" the way they do "That is the question" with the air of having invented something good.

Dearly do the English love an original. Charles Peace, said to have been the most respectable and to have played the organ in church, was the most beloved of Victorian murderers: as late as 1945 I heard an Army sergeant mutter of a little-loved officer, "Looks like Charley Peace dressed up." An eccentric with a good turn of phrase finds in reality or fiction a quick path to immortality. Consider Sam Butler; nobody today has heard of him, no one has read *The Way of All Flesh* but everyone knows Mr. Pontifex. "I have named the child Ernest, I have baptised him in water from the Jordan, and his father cannot tell the difference between a cock and a hen lobster." My citations are from memory and probably all slightly wrong; the point is that one knows them by heart.

We approach too the heart of the matter. The English in late Victorian times ruled the world and let everybody know that it was by force of personality. No great violence was needed; rumbustious phrases sufficed to keep the Pax Britannica. If insolent outsiders, French or American, got at all uppity, then a pithy word silenced them. Edward VII, invited to inspect the huge new naval works at Kiel, the menacing German fleet, began his speech of thanks, "Our shared interest in yachting . . ." Probably the Widow at Windsor never said, "We are not amused," but the invention is perfect; the resounding snub roundly delivered. It worked. Alfred Austin, the utterly ludicrous Poet Laureate, spouts jingoist boastfulness in every utterance, but the Brits believed it and the world stood bemused: our cool-headed bulldog Briton could subjugate any howling mob of foreigners. It even worked with lesser, while white still and even Brit, breeds. Did Mr. Baldwin really say "Run along now" to the trade unions?—one wouldn't be a bit surprised.

The Brit gutter press maintains the legend to this day. When Diego Maradona cried after losing a football match this was proof of his being a great sissy as well as a disgusting animal; a great gormless Brit boy started to blubber and became an instant saint: our lads have such warm hearts.

Holmes embodies all this effortless superiority. Police forces are a continental invention and we take a dim view. People like Lestrade (even the name is Frog) are arrogant and incompetent: not English, objects Mr. Podsnap. To underline this, European crowned heads beat a path to Holmes' door, their police being nitwits and their advisers indiscreet. It is only fair to add that the same kindly condescension extends to English dukes and grave statesmen, all rather thick in the wits. It will culminate in 1914, when diabolical Huns are sent scuttling. Thereafter other godlike men of few words, like Richard Hannay and General Haig, will have to bear the burden of Brit supremacy: they aren't quite as good at it. The legend is tenacious. Plenty of otherwise quite sensible English people believe to this day that the downfall of the Empire came about only because Burgess and Maclean knew secrets in High Places.

The confusion of fictional characters with reality is a psychological truism. A pregnancy is invented for the heroine of some pulpy television series?—floods of baby clothes will arrive at the studio. No special talent is called for. The actress can sign her fictional name to columns of advice to young girls, written for a magazine by a public relations man, and be believed. Other than Holmes, I know of no instance where this belief has been world-wide, and maintained for so long. That little house in Baker Street—dispiriting thoroughfare—is like the shrine at Lourdes. Americans from Iowa jostle starry-eyed Japanese on the dingy pavement, and solemnly take photographs. This is surely remarkable? It is not imaginable anywhere else in the world: only the English have the capacity so to transmute myth into reality. Nobody in St. Petersburg is going to point to a house saying, "Prince Pierre lived there"; there is no plaque on a wall in Paris to say "La maison du Père Goriot." Even in London, where they are so given to taking the wish for the reality, nobody says "This was Soames Forsyte's office." The hold of Doyle's creation is unique.

Holmes was to have innumerable subsequent avatars, some a bit odd. For if most, like Philo Vance or Sexton Blake, are merely lifeless wooden copies while some like Charlie Chan at least managed to be amusing, quite a few can be called downright pernicious. A Holmes copy can always be recognised, however dressed up; he is a wealthy amateur, and frequently of the leisured class, with nothing else to do and boasting highly placed relations and aristo connections. He has eccentric habits and mannerisms. And he is a Superman. Nero Wolfe is a good example. Some variations on the theme show ingenious inversions, like Father Brown, apparently unpretentious until he starts to talk. But the superhuman quality, the ability to reach out from a languid slippered ease to collar the malefactor, would quite shortly give rise to some nasty and even downright fascist examples. These are not merely snobbish or anti-Semitic, in the modern sense racist, but show a really disgusting readiness to disregard all process of law: they use their social, physical, or intellectual superiorities quite crudely to pop out and zap anyone of whom they disapprove. Examples are the Four Just Men, or Bulldog Drummond, or the Saint.

I said "pernicious" because although these figures are childishly simplistic, rarely above the comic-strip level, that is just the point; they appeal to the adolescent mentality. This sounds priggish—like frowning upon little boys who go "Da-da-da" with plastic machine guns, as of course they all do. But behind the zap-blonk stuff is some very specious reasoning, and this also appeals to little boys. It can be summed up as the Robin Hood syndrome. I am an outlaw and can do as I please. You, the villain, are too cunning and/or too well protected for the law to apprehend or punish you. Ergo, I decide to zap you; I am God-ordained to do so, you being a filthy Jew, Wog, or Commie. This is abject as well as vicious, basically so, since it avoids all notion of responsibility. These people answer to no one (an unconvincing cover may be given by some shadowy secret-service chief). They enjoy great privilege and lead lives of material ease and riches: they get the girls, are thanked by the Minister, ennobled by the Queen, and are admired by all right-thinking folk. The little boys bask in such fantasies and no wonder. Conan Doyle would have been horrified, but Holmes, ultimately, is responsible, and must answer for much of it.

Holmes himself illustrates, and be it said, very brilliantly, Mannerism; a familiar phenomenon in discussing art. It is to be seen in all the outstanding new departures, and Gothic architecture is a classic example. The new energy follows a rising curve, stays at a peak of achievement through it may be a century, and begins to fail. At this point, and the progress of nineteenth-century prose fiction provides a parallel I am trying to view more closely in these essays, the artists search for new forms to prop up the movement's declining energy: these forms are Mannerist. The over-decorated curving stylisations of the Late Gothic era are efforts to compensate for the lost simplicity and natural strength of earlier work: the hip-shot sexy madonnas of the fourteenth century have none of the forthright sturdiness of the thirteenth. After Balzac, Zola, and after Flaubert, Maupassant; in the last third of the nineteenth century one can see prose fiction turning to Mannerism. The novelty of Poe struck the French as invigoratingly original, yet it was only an exaggerated stylisation. A flock of vigorous and imaginative scribblers, Leroux or Ponson du Terrail, enjoyed themselves frightening the bourgeoisie with "shocking" sub-Zola inventions; bogeymen who flitted in at fourth-floor windows and stole the jewellery before disappearing into the gothic catacombs.

Dickens himself, the progress of whose career is so remarkable, was to fall into the new Mannerism.

He was, admittedly, at the end of his overcharged and electrified life, and to populate a tale he laid hold of phantoms quite as preposterous as the early, immature Fagins and Quilps. I hope, in this book, to defend my contention that Dickens in maturity is among the finest of crime novelists, but by the time of *Our Mutual Friend* the four books that show him at his peak were behind him: he was physically ill as well as deeply neurotic. The evocation of the river as the great sewer is still magnificent. The golden dust, a monstrous shit-heap that in central London still towered up as threatening as Vesuvius, is—almost—as good as the Marshalsea, but the force and the satiric edge are lost in sentimentalism; all agree that this is a steep sad falling-off. As for *The Mystery of Edwin Drood* nobody (bar as always the French) can take it seriously for a second; it is third-rate Fantomas. One is glad, and relieved, that it should be unfinished: it is trash. The alternative solutions are mere academic witterings: it is obvious that Jasper will be brought to book through a melodramatic mechanism involving Durdle and Deputy. Helena Landless, like all of Dickens' women, is without real dimension: she may promise, but she won't perform.

My discontent with the Holmes stories (a more heavyweight word would be inappropriate) is precisely that they fall within the feeble conventions defined in *Drood*. The bright young man, cut off in his golden years; that other bright young man so obviously given a motive (high words have passed) for making away with him: Edwin and Neville, stock Victorian figures, will pop up again and again in the Doyle canon. So will the rosebud young woman beset by suitors whose motives are to be distrusted, and the other young woman in straitened circumstances. There are lots of respectable personages with guilty secrets and, of course, people who sneak about in disguises; that elderly gentleman with the flowing grey hair. Minor stock figures will be uncorked ad hoc; bluff young sailor with the frank open face, pompous commercial gent, shrewd old lawyer.

Dickens in decline is a great artist still, and if what there is of *Drood* is poor stuff, *Our Mutual Friend* is from an unmistakable hand, were it only one line, like the young man who says "Esker." One thinks of Jenny Wren's streetwise study of fashionable ladies, Fledgeby feeling for his whiskers, Riderhood's rescue from drowning, or the Bird of Prey's navigation technique. My especial fondness is for Wegg drinking tea with Mr. Venus; many will agree. This is the very stuff of Victorian London and Doyle neglects it altogether. We are told that Holmes is the great authority upon the underworld but this is quite unconvincing; the compass is as narrow as Galsworthy's. The splendid old man who loses his goose exists only for Holmes to hold forth about his hat.

The objections are familiar: that these are brief stories with no room for character, which would unbalance the episode. Quite so; my complaint is not against the stories, which of their kind are unmatched, but against the solemn canonisation. Magazine tales should be seen in their context. The Metropolitan Line chunters from Baker Street to Harrow in exactly the

right time for reading "Silver Blaze." Splendid, but the deifica-
tion has elevated some very thin contrivances to awestruck status. Colonel Moran we are told is a great criminal but his only
source of revenue appears to be cheating at cards, which is
poor pickings. A silly young man has him taped after a few
nights of play, while the police continue to be all at sea. How
could one possibly suspect a senior officer of the Indian Army,
and famous big-game shot to boot? Sad stuff, this. But never
mind; the contrivance of the air-gun is what we remember—
the ambush in the empty house, the eye along the sights, the
little sigh, the tinkle of broken glass. What? Rickmansworth
already?

At their best—swift, spellbinding—they are magnificent
inventions. I want my flesh to creep. What do I care for the
clumsiness of the change of bedrooms? Why worry if Doctor
Grimesby Roylott—marvellous name—has brought his snake
all the way here (and kept it in a safe, poor thing) expressly to
bite young girls who have financial expectations? That gentle
hiss as of steam from a kettle makes up for all. I sit back in a
stalls seat of the Edwardian theatre and feel my neck prickle. I
am absolutely delighted when Holmes' ridiculous *mise en
scène,* a handful of straw and a shout of fire, makes the wicked
builder pop out of his secret cubby-hole. Even if it is all so la-
boriously over-elaborate, even if I cannot believe for a second
that the young man with the twisted lip could manage his tran-
sition into a pathetic beggar so pat and glib with a bit of soot
and a scrap of sticking-plaster: there has been a flash of genius,
and that's what I call it.

No, for Holmes I have nothing but admiration. What worries me is the half-century wasted in copying him. In a five-
minute story these melodramas captivate me. Erected, thirty
years later, into a whole book, they are fatuous trash. Professor

Moriarty is called a Napoleon of crime. Doyle never gives the slightest evidence to back this up; we don't care that he went on and on disappearing through secret trapdoors, hissing in frustration as yet another governess escapes a frightful fate in Buenos Aires, thanks to the Saint. It is not as though there existed no good crime fiction during these fifty years; there was plenty. But the whole world would be so stunned by the Holmes phenomenon that imitative tripe would be written in immeasurable quantity and greeted with rapture: why?

Holmes embodies the manifest superiority of the Empire over the subject peoples of the globe. A great many Britons cannot overcome their nostalgia for those years. A great many Americans cannot come to terms with their dream of world-wide domination (Lord Salisbury, who had more sense, defined the administration of the Empire as drifting gently downstream with here or there a touch upon the rudder). In several other countries dictators whose reading is confined to armament catalogues fall into a gentle doze; they have seen James Bond films, but these too are in thrall to Holmes.

It was all a marvellous confidence trick; the man who sold the Eiffel Tower for scrap. All these dukes, titled ladies, ministers, and millionaires who come running to Holmes in desperate straits—they are all fraudulent and the slightest, Orwellian touch of common sense dispels the illusion. Untold millions go on believing in it.

Doyle himself—there is a photograph of him, tweed-suited bourgeois gentleman in middle age, kindly, sensitive, a decent man. He stands on the platform at Waterloo, about to usher his two small boys into the train which will bring them to another term at Tonbridge or Sherborne: play the game and avoid masturbation. Upon these two little boys rests the future of the Empire and, poor wretches, they believed it too. I did myself, at the age of eight; my mother was madly in love with Paul Robeson and went five times to see *Sanders of the River.* Watching that magnificent man standing in his canoe singing—so well—delightful tripe about how happy they all were being ruled by Sandi the Good, Sandi the Wise, one was quite sure that this vaguely Cheltenham figure (the actor Leslie Banks was another decent man, bearing a faint resemblance to Conan Doyle) would indeed rule for all eternity. Sherlock Holmes was steering the canoe.

✤

❧ *Rudyard Kipling*

IN THE EARLY 1930s, when I was still a small child, my parents were in the habit of borrowing a holiday cottage on Burwash Common in the summer months. I became aware that just down the road lived a great magician. He was then a very old magician; invisible, and there could be no question of invading the privacy so precious to him all his days. One made do, as he had bid, with what he had written. Thus the words spoken by Una to Puck, "But that's Willingford Bridge. We go for walks there, often," had a particular resonance. So did we. This lump of land was Pook's Hill. The brook in the valley, in which we played, was, though I did not know that, Friendly Brook. It was the earliest of literary influences and being psychological has remained the strongest. An emotional tie as strong as the intellectual understanding that comes with maturity has always been of great importance in apprehending this particular magician.

That Kipling is a very great writer is no longer in any doubt. Max Beerbohm, who hated him, is a faded footnote in the history of the Aesthetic movement. The political theories, in their day so sore an obstacle to many, have melted into oblivion, Kipling remains the outstanding artist in English prose between 1890 and today. Perhaps a stamp, set in childhood, is important to the Kipling critic: the best of them, Miss J. M. S. Tompkins (in *The Art of Rudyard Kipling*, to which I am much indebted), remembered finding a Rowntrees Clear Gum used as a bookmark. Sixty years later I have read and reread, through the whole arc of my life educating and enriching; distilling too, so that a particular story of great vividness and power seen in the light of youth takes on quite another meaning late in life.

I am called a crime novelist; to many people still that is thought a trivial thing, and the theme as trivial. The view is understandable, since a great deal of so-called crime writing is indeed trivial, but to so generalise the definition is a grave error. The majority of writers work upon crime themes, since here they find the richest raw material for their purpose, which is to throw light upon human endeavour and the ways of the human spirit. Since Kipling is still thought of as primarily a writer about India, the random example that comes to my mind is Paul Scott's long but fine *Quartet*. It will be remembered that the basic anchorage-point of this immense book is the alleged rape of a white girl by a young Indian man: in the historical context there could be no greater crime, and that in fact it is not so is irrelevant, for the book is about the emotions aroused by the doubt. Between England and India there is a complex and difficult love story, and rape is a fundamental element in this, upon both sides.

Thus too we look at Kipling's major contemporaries, Henry James and Joseph Conrad, and we find unambiguous crime stories. Sometimes there is physical violence; we can find both rapes and murders. More often we can find a subtle interior destruction of a human being which we could call spiritual or psychological; there is indeed a strongly metaphysical element within these themes. A child or a woman in particular can be murdered without any physical bloodshed. Perhaps the locus classicus here is Madox Ford's still greatly underestimated novel *The Good Soldier*; Graham Greene, a most remarkable expert, did not make this mistake.

It would thus be crassly insensitive to denigrate Kipling's handling of crime themes. The magician could master any subject that came to his hand, from the earthiest farce to technical visions of the future, which we now call science fiction. His range is exceptional and often he combines themes so that they are not immediately apparent. We recall his famous image of close-packed bales of stuff whose texture would not be seen unless unwound, and held to the light . . .

Throughout his career, crime themes are never far away; closest to the surface in his beginnings, where many tales deal with violence, destruction, and despair, and towards the end, when there is no corner of the human heart unknown to him, and no suffering unfamiliar. What are we to make of the great masterpieces of his late work? The themes of love and crime are inextricably intertwined.

He even amused himself with a detective story! Even if "Fairy-Kist" is a minor tale I cite it as an instance of his technical mastery, so impressive to any professional writer.

I wish to examine, in slightly more depth, three of his stories chosen from what a chess player might call his openings (his reputation rested originally upon the dash and audacity of his early work); his middle-game (as every critic has noticed, much flawed and psychologically blocked, which goes far to explain the violence and rigidity of his political opinions); and his incomparable end game. This provides a balance. So that I intend to speak of "Love o' Women," taken from the early Indian tales; "Friendly Brook," among the shortest and most perfect of his late tales; and yes, in the middle, we find a much abused and much questioned tale, which has caused much bitter warfare among the critics and the lovers and is to this day a subject of aggravated controversy—that beautiful and haunting tale, "Mrs. Bathurst." Perhaps of all his stories this one is the closest to my heart.

"Love o' Women" is a poor title, but a very fine story. Anybody would be proud to have written it; and nobody else could. It has all the Kipling signatures, the energy, the technical mastery, the startling originality like a punch—so richly deserved—in Mr. Beerbohm's mincingly malicious eye. And to be sure, all the failings of the young Kipling, as detailed in that squeaky, precious mouth, are there also. The noisy knowingness, the cocky assurance, the coarse and vulgar assumption that the young Kipling who understood every secret was in the confidence of all, from the Viceroy down. Most of the early stories suffer from this, that the experience of adult men and women is conveyed to us corrected and improved upon by a boy of nineteen. Mulvaney is old in the sudden and terrifying ways of India. What could the little journalist boy know of a man like that—able to take the responsibilities of any of his seniors, including his officers, indeed often promoted, and broken again for drunkenness? What could the puppy grasp of the secret emotional life of a woman like Dinah Shadd?

Objections have often been made to Mulvaney's preposterous stage Irish. The fault here, I think, lies not so much with Kipling's ear as with the generalised tragic insensitivity of all Englishmen towards Ireland. We may disregard this, to ask more pertinently how he got everything else right. The answer is of course that the horrid little boy was a genius; as well ask how the young Mozart . . . ? As far as we know, the boy had never seen a shot fired in anger, and that—justly world-famous—opening paragraph of "Love o' Women" is as though written by a police reporter of thirty years' standing. Scarcely a man jack is today alive to tell us how the bugle call sounded, across the parade ground at Mian Mir. We do not need the eyewitness. We know. This blaze and incandescence of imagination, in a technique learned from the Robert Brown "Mr. King" threw at the schoolboy's head, will cover much.

Not quite enough: as we will see, the story has grave flaws, masterpiece of crime writing though it is. The terror, which even Mulvaney can barely apprehend, is largely lost on the young Kipling, though the genius can seize, unseeing, on what we now know. Larry is a gentleman-ranker, a crucifyingly painful fate. An Irishman, and the combination holds slow screws of torment that even Mulvaney can only guess at. The charming Paddy, who can seduce any woman he lays eye upon. It comes to us through the filters of two imperfect observers; Mulvaney who can see half, and Kipling who is frankly out of his depth. Larry knows that he is in the third stage of syphilis; it is paralysing him, and will shortly kill him. Among the women he has ruined (we are not told whether she is physically infected, though it is likely) is one who has now sunk to common prostitution but who means everything to him; she is his "Diamonds and Pearls." She too is a woman of education, and will recognise the allusion when he tells her, "I am dying, Egypt, dying." Unfortunately, this is mawkish.

Mawkishness in prose occurs when the writer's technical ability to convey lyricism cannot keep pace with the lyricism of imagination; it is the case here: we cannot quite believe in the harlot who has read Shakespeare. She can, though, have the splendour to say "Die here" and to join him in death. Mulvaney remarks shrewdly that only an exceptional woman will have the courage to use a pistol. We can forgive the little lapse into sentimentalism. In a realistic tale, such as those of

Maupassant, fatally second-rate, we would reject it. Here there is a metaphysical truth to the double death, recognised by the army doctor who will pay for the two to be buried together, and we accept it.

The blemish has little impact upon the story, which as a whole is magnificently written. That opening paragraph has been singled out by every Kipling commentator. I can say with confidence that it is unsurpassed anywhere; perhaps un-equalled because (speaking as a professional in the trade) those seven spare sentences are technically incomparable: the plain language brings to the reader the violence of a blood crime as none other has. The cinema can convey this abrupt immediacy, but words create a barrier nigh insuperable. The dried blood cracks lozenge-wise, curls "like a dumb tongue." The de-tached, distancing comment, "It was too hot to stand in the sunshine before breakfast." The smith cooling the white-hot metal. And last, that spaced, deliberate cadence, "shrieked and raved with wicked filthy words." He is no longer nineteen; the story is from the *Many Inventions* collection. But this writer is still in his early twenties.

One can turn the page and find the jarring, characteristic fault. "What the trial would be like I knew even to weariness," made still worse by the irritating archaism, and it will take Ortheris' retort to the damned-impudent-little-lawyer before we have quite forgiven the little reporter. Crime, trial, sentence in five harsh, heat-blistered pages, and where will we find an-other five to set beside them? It is the frame in which Kipling sets his picture, and since Mulvaney's tale of the gentleman-ranker is very terrible, both frame and picture have a sledge-hammer impact.

The reporter remarks that the Irishman has been on a good few of these prisoners' guards, and the answer comes "Scores

of them" with a "worn smile," and in those two monosyllables
we are told that Mulvaney has himself been within a hairsbreadth of killing or of being killed on the same account; a tale
of womanising has the more force from a man whose experience is hard bought. We will find the same technique at work
in "Mrs. Bathurst"—the two sailors know all about picking up
barmaids in distant harbours—and in the totally mature tale of
"Friendly Brook"; the two Sussex woodsmen know that they
would act, in similar circumstances, very much as has Jim
Wickenden. Mulvaney has escaped the fate of Corporal
Mackie, shot for seducing another man's wife, and of Larry,
who dies of syphilis, by the thinnest of margins. "He'll have
got shot of amusements, except turning from one side to the
other, these few years to come." In the heavy deliberate sentence is the whole life of the private soldier in Victorian India,
lying on the barrack cot with nothing to do until it was time for
beer, since the work had to be done in the relative cool of early
morning. Whoever was cursed with imagination saw devils; or
with education, planned devilry. Ortheris and Learoyd like
Mulvaney's stories, since they pass the time. Kipling has left a
vivid drawing of the night guard, stripped to the waist and sitting up to avoid heat stroke. India was a land where a man
healthy in the early morning could be dead within twenty-four
hours, and they all knew it.

Browning's famous phrase about the dangerous edge of
things has been overworked, but we still live in a world where a
man can take a woman seriously. He can kill her, and for her;
we had better not forget that. Today's reporters are as blasé
and, in their own estimation, as worldly wise as ever was Kipling. Beneath the frothy soufflé of today's journalism, the need
at all cost to be Amusing, one can still find heartbreak and
tragedy. Kipling's sleight-of-hand, that this is all good

smoking-room stuff, to pass the time abaft the funnel on a liner between Capetown and Southampton, must not deceive us. The tales are full of blood and terror, and amongst them we can find some of the finest crime writing in a century.

Larry has seduced the Colonel's governess, and the Major's maid. We think nothing of that. Were it the Colonel's wife, what of it? But Larry is a private, the lowest form of life in white-skinned India. A man could fancy a bit-of-brown. In 1890 the barriers made a love affair impossible between an Indian man and a white woman, such as Paul Scott has described. But an officer's wife and a soldier? If it could happen it would not be spoken of. Many things were not spoken of, including European prostitutes, and Diamonds and Pearls is nigh-fatally occulted and sentimentalised, as were the prostitutes in Dickens.

We must give Kipling his due; "Love o' Women" is in the collection bracketed between "Brugglesmith," the blackest of his farces, and "Badalia Herodsfoot," in which a woman is kicked to death as Sikes kicks Nancy, and despite a lot of Salvation Army pieties we don't have to guess what happens. "Come to bed," Badalia asks of her dreadful man, and she meets her death with the nobility of Desdemona. But it was still impossible for a writer to approach some subjects without detour. Kipling builds his picture of Larry's approaching death with much technical skill—but it's very long! For five pages of dialogue (as long as "the frame"), Mulvaney seems annoyingly slow to catch on to Larry's trouble, which a Victorian doctor called "G.P.I."—general paralysis of the insane, or tertiary syphilis untreated. We suspect, too, that Kipling is taking undue pleasure in a protracted description of Stalky tactics in irregular warfare. However, Mulvaney sums it up well.

"Thanks to me, no casualties and no glory"—a modern, that is to say unsentimental, view of a frontier campaign.

Thereafter comes a three-page episode (but we should remember that a page in the standard Macmillan edition comes in large print and with unfashionably generous margins) in which the doctor tells us what is amiss with Larry. It took me some time to catch on when I first read this story, but I was fifteen. Since Mulvaney is not obtuse we must find him disconcertingly innocent: venereal disease was the army's great obsession. We will find it harder to forgive Kipling for weakening the impact with three more pages of sentimental tripe about the band playing as the regiment returns to base. It is quite unnecessary to tell us that Dinah Shadd and the Colonel's wife are honest women. The mature Kipling would have cut all this guff.

The conclusion still has the power to move us. Even the melodrama can move us.

When Diamonds and Pearls, such as Larry has thrown away with both hands, says "Here. Die here," I was emotionally moved, at fifteen years old: if I am moved at sixty-five there are metaphysical reasons for my tears. I am looking back, but stripped of self-pity. We can dismiss the little scratch-and-mew of the etiolated Beerbohm malice. We can say that there are technical flaws in this marvellous story, much that needs cutting and tightening (as would be done in maturity to "Friendly Brook"). Especially, we would say, after those incomparable five first pages; for the ending, back in "the frame," with Ortheris the successful perjurer whistling, "That's what the girl told the soldier" is perfunctory. We can look at this fine crime story with profit to ourselves.

"Love o' Women" would be rich enough nowadays to

develop—in other hands—into a novel. Larry's seductions of young girls and married women would not today be counted as crime fiction; a trivial episode—would we say?—in everyday existence. If there is a crime it is the deliberate infection with syphilis. Today the writer would remark that man or woman knowing themself HIV positive and recklessly continuing to seek sexual partners was indeed behaving "with criminal intent." I agree, but argument is beside the point. I would argue that women continue to suffer agonies on account of the handy male myth that women enjoy promiscuity. But in 1890, Larry is simply a moral murderer; his syphilis is an evangelical punishment, a foretaste of hell. We may notice in passing that Badalia absolves "her man" of responsibility. Before slipping into the coma that precedes death she will still maintain, "Nobody; I myself." What writer has given us the heroism of the raped and battered Victorian wife? Galsworthy? As well say Mickey Mouse. Poor dear Henry James? As well cite Lewis Carroll. Dickens? Ellen Ternan does not, will not, cannot say.

A melodramatic climax to a tale is judged by what went before: are the characters able to carry the reader to, and through it? Kipling does not always meet this test, but here there can be no doubt, I believe. Ortheris planning perjury, staring at the prosecutor—"a nasty little baldheaded butcher"—is never better; and in no other Mulvaney story is this battered, failed man behind the experience and authority so convincing. The drunken doctor's cynical talk is nicely attuned—but the two principals?

The gentleman-ranker is admirably drawn. This, in Victorian India, was a tragic destiny and perfectly motivates his crimes. His isolation is shown in one line: "You're getting very quick on your feet," he tells Mulvaney during the fight. "Among gentlemen that's called no pretty name." Quick comes the retort "Among privates it's different." Everything combines to cut Larry off from survival; only in crime can he find himself.

We have more doubt about Diamonds and Pearls. We have only Larry's word that she is exceptional. We are not told her status; is she married or single? She has some education, and strength of purpose, and is clear-sighted. She rides out on horseback to meet the regiment and we may guess that she is the madam rather than one of the girls. She has taken to prostitution through self-disgust rather than economics—"You always said I was a quick learner." Plainly she too is a gentleman-ranker; it is the basis of her understanding with Larry that she has been a lady.

About the story as a whole there is no doubt: it has the inevitability of good crime writing. The knowingness is a flaw and in part it is badly overwritten: the immature and insecure Kipling is too anxious to convince us that he had seen a regiment in battle and the dilapidated savagery of its return to cantonments. There is more, and it is fine, of much beauty, and dare one say—nobility.

Kipling's middle period is the subject of much misunderstanding. An effort is needed to get these years into perspective. In the context of his career as a writer, there is one date important beyond all the others: 1899, a terrible, traumatic year.

It is almost impossible for us now to imagine, and thus understand, the scene. He went down himself with pneumonia, in a hotel, after a bad Atlantic crossing in midwinter. He very nearly died. The press was completely hysterical. People prayed for him in the street. He was the world's most famous writer, and the wealthiest, but neither Pope nor President would get those headlines now. He recovered, and it was all forgotten. But not by him: while he had slowly recovered, his daughter Josephine, the light of his eye and the breath of his being, herself also stricken with pneumonia, had died. Kipling never fully recovered.

Nearly ten years passed before his Sussex home gave him again some contentment and peace; and even this was to be brutally broken by the death of his son at Loos in 1915. But from that dreadful moment in New York (never again would he see the United States) date the dotty politics and extreme reactionary views. Humanly, he was flung into a sort of deep freeze and the recovery, I repeat, was never entire. Artistically, the nigh deathwound was to serve him. He would create the incomparable work of his late period. He had great resources.

His fame, and wealth, crowned by a Nobel Prize, meant little. (Money was handy; he could buy anything he fancied; he could and did spend ten winters in the sun of South Africa.) There was his wife, Carrie. Whatever her faults she was the strongest and toughest mainstay. There was at last his home, his place; his stillness and his peace with himself. After false starts in Torquay, in Rottingdean, he found in Burwash a cure to the insecurity expressed in that crying need for calm, for privacy, for space to breathe. He never stopped writing, and indeed these years give us *Kim,* his farewell to India, a magnificent expression of the acceptance he imposed upon himself— the discipline, and finally the serenity—still thought of by many as a crowning achievement. And two bumpily uneven collections of stories: *Actions and Reactions* and *Traffics and Discoveries*; the titles speak to his awareness. The genius had taken a dreadful blow and a major check. He would fight his way out.

For he had also his matchless technique. The family-square of his early years was broken; his father died during these years, and his gifted sister Trix relapsed into intermittent insanity. His home in Vermont was lost and his own family life shattered, but his pen, he knew now, could do anything. He could handle any theme he chose to submit to his skills. It is within this context that we must view these two collections. They are astoundingly varied: even at their worst the flare of imaginative force is most impressive.

It gives the opening paragraph of "The Captive," as good as anything he ever wrote. It gives "The Bonds of Discipline" and "Their Lawful Occasions," generally seen as insupportably facetious but, as I prefer to believe, a delight in embellishing farce with purple prose; overwritten, but the best overwriting there is. It is indeed neurotically intense when compared to the later "Vortex," but this new-found passion for the Royal Navy is like the over-engagement in South African politics: a means of hiding his heart from abiding pain. Pyecroft's fantasies would grate upon us were it not for a sudden vision that the same histrionic imagination could also perceive tragedy, and this we get, in the story of Mrs. Bathurst.

The story is a reef on which every critic has run aground.

*

Miss J. M. S. Tompkins and other critics have recognised it as a masterpiece but seen it as flawed by apparent obscurity and what has generally been viewed as overreaching cutting. Others, I can only call them crassly insensitive, see nothing at all, and ask what all the fuss is about. There are many questions that open troubling vistas and pinch, acutely; one cannot pass them by. To me this story is among Kipling's half-dozen finest, and I find no insuperable difficulties. The cutting I agree to be brutal. He was a most expert cutter, and once we accept that he intended the cutting to be ferocious, the better to illuminate a ferocious aspect of human behaviour, the difficulty vanishes. It has given rise to some wildly inconsequent misinterpretations. Faced with a tragic tale of passion, many and many a Court of Assizes has made the same mistake.

South Africa—four other tales in the collection have this setting, but here the bright light, the heat, the exotic fruits and flowers, the harshly vivid colours have extra weight and resonance. For Pyecroft, Simonstown has more stimulus as a setting than Plymouth. Only at the end will he need to finish what's left of the beer. A particularity of the story is that it contains elements taken from all over the globe—Auckland and Vancouver as well as London and Cape Town. The Simonstown navy base gives a clear, coherent focus to the sailors' recollections.

Pyecroft himself in his stagey, flowery language seems too frivolous a personage for a tale of this dramatic intensity, but I believe he supplies a needed dimension. We have here not one "imperfect narrator" but three, and they are cunningly contrasted: the voluble and articulate Pyecroft with the stolid but emotionally sensitive Pritchard and meticulous, unimaginative Inspector Hooper. Commonplace events are filtered through an exotic, fantastical imagination, and the tragedy will gain in impact. Pritchard is the necessary corrective, while Inspector Hooper is only concerned with facts. One would almost be tempted into thinking him a deliberate parody of the Lestrade type of detective (Kipling knew and was friendly with Conan Doyle). The humourless earnestness of carrying Vickery's false teeth around in his pocket is a particularly nice touch. Kipling's approach, thus, to the enigma is not crassly complicated, as has often been thought, but of great subtlety.

Crime stories of this complexity and force demand treatment at full length. An outstanding example is Madox Ford's *Good Soldier.* Kipling's characteristic method of compression and elimination gives us the tragedy neat, which is like drinking whisky straight from the bottle. There is none of the sentimental brutality of the Maupassant manner, but it hits very hard. "Finish what's left of the beer and thank God he's dead," we will say with Pyecroft at the end.

The Vancouver passage, often thought irrelevant, illustrates the innocence of these Navy men who think themselves worldly-wise because they have travelled in obscure corners of the world, but are susceptible to a glamorous fantasy. They were all court-martialled but they looked back upon the episode with relish. Just this touch of glamour and fantasy is the key to Mrs. Bathurst herself. She is unforgettable, yet we hardly see her. She pervades the whole scene (made deliberately worldwide) with the strength of her personality. She is perfectly respectable, looks—we may guess—quite ordinary, but possesses strong sexual attraction, seen through the few inarticulate words in which Pritchard describes her. Hooper, albeit with sympathy, "doesn't really see her yet"—but Kipling has! She has "It," a catchword later much employed for movie stars: the mysterious quality that gives an ordinary pretty face the magnetism felt through the screen, without a physical presence. One must emphasize screen because of that amazing passage in which Mrs. Bathurst is glimpsed with her "blindish look," clutching her handbag—the hair prickles at it. "She's looking for me"—and Vickery must get drunk night after night, alone with his vision and the knowledge of what it portends, forcing Pyecroft to share his solitude and guess at the reasons for the need of alcoholic oblivion; terrifying him—for Pyecroft has imagination, and some idea of her innocence, and her dreadful power.

We must also make an effort. This complaint—that Kipling is fumbling, that abrupt cuts, irritating obscurities, the jerks and blurs in the narration bespeak failure—is that at all likely? This supreme technician? Who, moreover, would keep a story back for years, working at it, before judging it fit for publication? It is true that quite an early work, "Children of the Zodiac," an elaborately-wrought and rather artificial fable about the burden of pain and solitude laid upon the talented artist, is a semi-failure. It is true that "The Tie," thought worthy of inclusion in a late collection, is no better than a tetchy anecdote in Kipling's crudest schoolboy manner. Many of his stories fail to meet my tastes, fail to give me pleasure. I suppose that thus I must forgive Angus Wilson for his inability to see anything in this story. But surely this instance is simple enough. These are the characteristics of the early cinematograph, able to bring an audience out of its seats in sudden shock while still wavery, blurry, given to disconcerting changes of pace, and to breakdowns. I am certain, and serenely so, that the technique is deliberate; that we see Mrs. Bathurst the way we hear Caruso sing, see Sarah Bernhardt act, or listen to Yeats recite a poem.

A crime story; of its nature dark, terrible, and obscure. Two human beings are destroyed. We do not know why. We are not given to know because we must not know. We apprehend, exactly like the oafish crowd boozing in the pub in Auckland. "I assure you Mr. Hooper—even a sailorman has a heart to break." Mawkish? No. Consider her one line—one only—of direct speech: "Ada, fetch me Sergeant Pritchard's particular." Pritchard, that great lout, leans leering over the bar (his breath reeking of the particular) with the lumpiest compliment known. "Mrs. B.—you're my particular." So she is, for every one of us. Lightning strikes anywhere. Here it strikes Vickery. The affected and rather silly passage "from Lyden's 'Irenius'" is to me a flaw, Kipling's knowing nod-and-wink, telling us that an extraordinary woman happens to the milkman. On the screen it may be Clark Gable but in life it's this terribly ordinary man. A worse flaw to my mind is Kipling's overdoing it; Vickery is nicknamed Click because his false teeth do not fit well.

Is it difficult to swallow? Not in the light of later stories. "The Dog Hervey" and "Dayspring Mishandled" will show us aspects of sexual passion surprising from the pen of this so-disciplined Victorian gentleman. How did he know? Carrington, that prudent biographer and well under the thumb of the terrifying Mrs. Bambridge, insists that never, never, in over forty years of blamelessly virtuous marriage with strong-minded Carrie—I can accept this. But the Daemon could think otherwise.

I spoke of difficulties, saying I had none, but I find one, because Mr. Philip Mason is the most sensitive of Kipling critics, and I am unhappy to find myself in disagreement with him here. He thinks this a murder story and points to ambiguities in the text. Vickery threatens Pyecroft with death. Pye, at the solemn stage of drunkenness, has said, "Assuming murder was done, or attempted." Vickery will say that he is free of guilt towards his lawful wife—one must emphasize the "lawful" since she has died naturally, six weeks after the ship left England. But has he murdered Mrs. Bathurst? Mr. Mason adduces points that worry him, but I cannot find them convincing.

The first is that Vickery is on his way up the line, and that the touring cinema show is at Worcester, fifty miles along. "So that I will see her yet once again," he says. Certainly this can be read to mean that he does not expect to see her again in the flesh, but, I suggest, just as easily as an ironic comment on his obsessive nightly visits to Cape Town: the remark is made to

Pyecroft, his—by now—far from willing companion.

The other point is that Hooper refers to the second dead tramp as Vickery's "mate," a word used of a man, or at least of a male. I see no inconsistency. Finding two tramps along a railway line, one would certainly assume at first that both were men. But it is emphasized that the figures are barely recognisable as human; the charcoal is soaked by rain and the figures "fell to bits." Plainly, all readily identifiable features, hair, hands, or countenance, are destroyed by the lightning. Vickery himself can be recognised only by the false teeth, the feature ("Click") which everyone had noticed, and by a tattoo mark showing white on black. Of the second figure all that is said is that it is crouching, which would make it still more difficult to recognise as anything but vaguely androgynous. When we consider that Hooper would not be expecting a woman and has not even known of Mrs. Bathurst's existence up to this moment, the objection, thin at best, dissolves altogether. She would in any case have taken off her wedding-ring.

Further, I would adduce two powerful pieces of evidence that the second figure is indeed Mrs. Bathurst. Miss Tompkins, unhappy with the claim that this is a man, concludes her penetrating analysis by remarking "All I can say is that if it were so Kipling has used a very uncharacteristic technique." I would go much further. A fiction writer myself, with some thirty years of experience in these techniques, I can assure any reader that it is inconceivable to drag in a new figure, previously unheard-of, on the last page. The story is called "Mrs. Bathurst" and she is the major character throughout, the more vividly so for being scarcely seen. It is consistent with both Kipling's thought and narrative method that in these closing paragraphs she should be seen, physically, by a third and conclusive witness. Of her nothing is left but a mass of charred matter. She has

Rudyard Kipling

been devoured by the lightning stroke as she was by passi
is her and none other. She crouches, helpless now, at Vicl
feet. He is standing. Miss Tompkins is surely right to su
that in a moment of despair he has deliberately attracte
lightning. Up there, on the high veldt, electric storms are
paralleled intensity. Rider Haggard, Kipling's friend, wi
powerful passage in which two witch doctors stage a d
conditions such as these, upon a terrain rich in iron, usir
lightning as weapon . . .

The other piece of evidence—all of it circumstantial b
we need proof?—is that Pritchard is in no doubt of the
tity. He covers his face with his hands. "To think of her
her hair ribbon on my beer." There are worse epitaph:
Mason, honest man, admits this but writes it off; Pritch
still in love with her. That is just the point. Pritchard, thr
out, has the best emotional understanding of her. His i
gence is of the heart, and love does not lead him astray. K
is telling us that this ox-like man, stolid and unimagir
shows a truer, deeper comprehension than Pyecroft.

One point remains. In the centre of the narrative the
considerable technical difficulty. How is the narration
Vickery away from the ship in Cape Town, and place
thousand miles away up-country? Kipling works this ad
if in over-complicated fashion. Vickery seeks a private
view with the captain, and we are told that this severe ar
right martinet has subsequently a "court-martial face,"
will remind us of the Vancouver episode (when the
wander away in the bush in pursuit of a fantasy). But
more grave, "as though someone was to be hanged." N
however happens beyond Vickery's being sent—alone
country, on some vague mission to do with recovering s
wartime stores. Plainly, this is an administrative cov

What can Vickery have said to the captain? I am afraid that Mr. Mason's speculative reconstruction again fails to convince me. I find no difficulty in suggesting that Vickery tells the Captain he intends to desert his ship, and on account of a woman, and that there will be no stopping him. A senior warrant-officer, within a year of his pension! This, in the Navy, is of itself a fearful occurrence, a huge black eye for both ship and captain.

So the cover-up must be for the Captain to tell him, "You have played fair in warning me, and I'll play fair with you. Very well, desert. I won't pursue you, and I'll find a pretext for allowing you to go. But then you vanish; hear me? You will never again be seen or heard of. If I get to know of you in the Cape Province, I'll have you picked up by the military police, and you know the penalty for desertion." And Vickery accepts; for him the faithful servant, the thirty-year man, this is the final and irrecoverable step, but none other is possible. What has he been thinking of, night after night, getting drunk with Pyecroft after watching the forty-five seconds of Mrs. Bathurst on the cinema screen? That he has no other way out. To me this is the only possible course of events, and the only explanation of his appearance up-country, with Mrs. Bathurst, both disguised as tramps. They are fleeing towards Rhodesia, where Navy law will not run.

Objections have been made to this dénouement. Sober, sensible people have said that Vickery's wife is dead, that there is no suspicion of foul play; that there is no reason for him to desert. Nothing stops him marrying Mrs. Bathurst and living, peacefully, on his pension.

It won't do, I'm afraid. It won't do for a writer; it won't do for the woman who would never hesitate to put her foot on a scorpion. It won't do for the woman who after a lapse of years

could say "Ada, fetch me Sergeant Pritchard's particular"—the four bottles of special beer, marked with her hair-ribbon. It is too sober and too sensible.

For what is the whole theme and purpose of this story? That a good, a kind, an innocent woman can possess a dreadful and destructive power. Vickery has certainly been tempted to kill his wife. Every scrap of his behaviour shows him suffering, hideously, from mingled guilt and passion. He has not killed his wife but in the last pinch, along the railway line, he will be forced to kill himself—and her. It is the theme that runs throughout every tale in the collection of *Rewards and Fairies;* so different from the gentle innocence of the earlier *Puck* book. "What else could I do?"

Where had Kipling come across such a woman? He heard tell of her in Auckland; he may have caught a glimpse of her. An adumbration took shape in his mind, to crystallise, as is a writer's wont, years later. Does she not share some characteristics with another woman of iron who set her feet upon scorpions? Whom he knew? Whom he was to know better? With a woman of whose secret passions we know nothing, because he would never, never say. But who—we do know—would never, throughout her life, accept a compromise. With, in fact, the mother of his Josephine, his very own Carrie.

*

"Friendly Brook" is a brief tale. In the standard Macmillan edition, it occupies only sixteen pages, where "Mrs. Bathurst," a story generally seen as cut to the bone, and certainly a miracle of compression, takes up twenty-seven. It would be a mistake to see the tale as trivial or lacking in weight on this account; it is a fine piece of crime fiction, exceptionally well written even by the highest Kipling standards, and poses a neat metaphysical problem. It is not a great masterpiece, such as all agree "Wish House" to be. Both share the local Sussex background; involve and are narrated by villagers, those of Kipling's day, before 1914. They are largely untravelled and uneducated; they lead an inbred, dour life, secret and suspicious. Their high intelligence is that of the emotions, of rich and deep-rooted oral traditions, of intense attachment to their land, their earth, their water. An arrogant or snobbish man "parachuted" into their midst, as Kipling was at Burwash, might have judged them ignorant, hostile, and superstitious. A striking trait in his genius was that this man, himself so reserved and hidden, barricaded behind his need for privacy, which amounted at times to mania, closed off by his wealth and fame, loved them and understood them. It has been noticed how acute his ear was for the shuffling, blurry East Sussex talk. It has not been noticed enough how deeply he reached inside them. We are not here dealing with Mulvaneys or Pyecrofts who have the gift of the gab, but with a folk superficially inarticulate, good at reading between one another's lines.

"A smuggling, sheepstealing race," he said when he first came to live among them. Sullen and mistrustful; poaching and prevaricating; every one a born lawyer. A united front against all outsiders. How quickly he learned. In Vermont he had cultivated notabilities, and failed with the country people. He would not make the same mistake here. His dayspring had been mishandled; like the girl in "Gertrude's Prayer" he had been forced back upon himself and cut off. He never came totally to terms with the distortions of his own personality, and his genius can be seen the better for it in his writing. His eye and ear remained as sharp but by 1910 he had gained a new deep knowledge of the human heart.

Jim Wickenden is one of these Sussex locals; smallest of small farmers, with a few fields and a cow or two, all pretty scrawny. He lives by the brook, and access to his cottage is by a couple of rickety planks across it: then as now, no peasant—anywhere—would spend good money on bridging. I may remark in passing that Kipling knew all about the brook; it flooded his own garden every autumn and the lament for the rosebeds in "My Son's Wife" is his own.

Jim's slatternly wife has died, and his old mother keeps house for him. There are no children, but they have a foster-child from Doctor Barnardo; that pays five shillings a week, a lot of money, but that alone will not count so with these villagers. Mary is not an attractive child, but they have grown much attached to her, and Jim views her as his own. It is important to remember that this adoption is not legal. Mary's "real" father, a drunken good-for-nothing Londoner, remains her legal guardian, and here is the crux of this—so small—village drama.

The story is narrated by a neighbour who knows them well, to another from further off and for whom the more intricate detail must be filled in. These two elderly men are busy with an overdue hedging job. It is a foggy wet November, and the brook is flooding: the overgrowth of rubbishy trees and bushes along the bank threatens to slip and block the stream—a calamity, for the flood would then back up upon good valley land. Indeed, Jim Wickenden has left valuable hay stacked in a low-lying field, and Jabez, the further neighbour, remarks upon this, for it is threatened. The economy of Kipling's craftsmanship is such that he can tell the tale quicker than I can explain it.

Jesse, the nearer neighbour, has made the same remark to Jim, and he has let fall a phrase to us highly enigmatic. "The brook's been a good friend to me," he has said, "and if she be minded to make a snatch at my hay . . . " "She," they call the brook. This piece of local superstition, the appeasing of the water-spirit with a sacrifice—this is the metaphysical point we will be called upon to make note of. To judge? That will be a question we may ask ourselves; no more. Miss Tompkins found herself much tormented, wondering whether she had the right to ask such a question.

The work is done, the brook runs smoothly, the two old boys stop for their lunch break—in the middle of the field, for hedges, they think, are nests of treachery and eavesdropping. They are quite right. It is a tale of blackmail—and perhaps murder—which will at last come out.

Jesse explains. Mary's "London father" has been turning up with threats to exercise his legal rights. He was sent packing by Mary herself, but comes back to pester Jim, who has no taste for violence—he overdid things once, in a fight, and spent six months in Lewes jail for it. Jim has been twisted into paying blackmail, and this gets worse with every appearance of the scrounger, who drinks Jim's whisky (an article to be careful with) and cleans out his earnings. That can no longer be endured, but Jim has a hesitant character. A good workman, but no real woodsman, and when throwing a tree "he doesn't rightly decide where to lay it." This quality of indecision is costing him dear.

Jesse recurs to a situation much like the present. Undergrowth and worse have blocked a bend in the flooded brook. He is alone on this occasion but Jim, seemingly with nothing else to do, offers to help, openly admitting that the scoundrel has turned up again; he has lacked courage to face him, and has left to his tough old mother the nasty task of bargaining a payment. As they finish the job of clearance a floating obstacle comes down with the current. Jesse takes it for an old beehive; it proves to be the body of the scoundrel. Plainly he has slipped while drunk on the shaky bridge, fallen in, drowned.

Jim, understandably, shows no feelings of pity. He searches the dead man's pockets for the money extorted, remarking grimly that it is more than he had ever parted with, and tips the body back into the flood to be carried downstream, "for I've done with him." Jesse, sympathising, has no comment to make. On his own way home by way of the plank bridge he notices that the flood has indeed undermined the banks, but that the rickety affair is easily stabilised country-style with a couple of bricks wedged under. He offers the story, now, in explanation of that laconic phrase "the brook's been a good friend to me."

Kipling makes no further comment; we are to decide this matter for ourselves, on the basis of what he has already told us. It sounds simple enough, and would so appear at an eventual inquest on a man found drowned, downstream. People did indeed fall into the brook, which in floodtime could be formidable. Nobody would make much of it; the man was known to be a worthless character, hanging about scrounging, rather like Mr. Polly's "Uncle Jim." Probably drunk into the bargain. An enquiry, even if made, would not get far. Trust the Sussex peasants to have seen nothing. A village policeman might have asked a few questions, drawn a few conclusions, and decided—wisely—to let things lie. Are our tender urban consciences worrying us?

It is perfectly reasonable to take the question at Jim Wickenden's own valuation. He has been a good neighbour to the brook. She has known him long, and has done him a good turn by removing an awkward problem. Jim will now pay her back by letting her take his hay. Rural Sussex will find that quite normal, and so will Kipling, good metaphysician that he is. He accepts it in the last line of the story. "The brook's note had changed. It sounded now as though she were mumbling something soft." Not, this time, Jim's hay: is the brook muttering that she keeps her own secrets? Is it so? Has not Kipling gone out of his way to tell us that there is more to this, and has he not spelt out some clues, which any policeman knowing his job could readily recognise?

Has the man simply fallen in, after a heavy dose of Jim's whisky? Quite a lot is made of this whisky; we are told that it was good stuff, and expensive, and Jim holds the bottle up to the light, rather indignant that the dirty chap has drunk so much of it. Well, that's natural enough; any peasant is close with money. But did Jim perhaps loosen the planks himself, anticipating that the blackmailer would be lurching, none too steady on his pins? That would be an intent to homicide, but quite impossible to prove.

Did Jim actually push him in? There is a further possibility, that the old woman pushed him in, either with Jim's connivance, or that he, lurking about, saw her do it. Sussex would be silent on the question. For Kipling tells us, apparently gratuitously, that the old mother is deaf and dumb. She communicates by writing on a slate tied to her waist. Why is this important? Why is it important that she has given the ruffian more money than Jim ever did? Kipling never wastes detail of this sort.

Miss Tompkins admits that she cannot make up her mind: at times she is sure that the flood has loosened the bricks, and then again . . . For it does look ominous that Jim should have come along just then, "slouching along." "Be you minded to some help?" "Be you minded to turn to?" answers Jesse, very naturally. He can know nothing of what may have happened, but it does look as though Jim is constructing an alibi, and securing a witness to it. It can be objected that the body turns up only after the work is finished; an unspecified time but at least an hour or two. It can be answered that Jim, "slouching" along the bank, has seen the man drown and the body perhaps catch with some other flotsam on some snag in the brook's blocked bed. Is this remark that "the brook's been a good friend to me," laconic like all their talk, self-incriminating when taken literally? And isn't Jim a bit too unsurprised when the body comes washing down?

He is safe with Jesse, who will only say what he knows in the middle of a sodden field; then only to old Jabez, who understands such things. It is certain that these subtle, silent old woodsmen will be as the grave, towards any outsider. The old woman cannot speak, and Mary, with no cause to be loyal to the father who has never taken his responsibilities towards her, will say nothing. But at the least, we may guess, Jim has given the Friendly Brook some help and encouragement.

Quite a pretty little problem. Kipling may have heard of it as a reality—not, to be sure, from "old Hobden" but conceivably from his neighbour Colonel Feilden. He would not have felt any impulse to alert any CID. The thought is foolish, for they would have known better than to launch an enquiry. I was of the same mind when a London editor invited me to report upon the notorious "Affaire Gregory," which occurred close to my home in France. A child was found dead in the river; a relative was shot and killed; there was a squalid tale of anonymous letters. The mother came under strong suspicion but nothing was ever proved. Three successive criminal investigation teams broke their heads on this, and a young, well-meaning judge of instruction, zealous for justice but wanting in experience, was disgraced. I was right to refuse the assignment. Subsequent magistrates have drowned this dossier in paper-work.

For Jim Wickenden is a decent man, much devoted to the daughter who is his in all but legal shuffledom. If he invoked the water-spirit, a reality to the peasant mind from long before the invention of Christianity, who is going to start mouthing pedantic inanities about justice? It is enough that Kipling understood.

Three examples have been chosen, from Kipling's relatively rare explorations of crime themes. The first is simple enough: Ortheris will perjure himself blind to make sure that human rather than legal justice is done: "Love o' Women's" atrocious death atones for his atrocious life, and the woman's voluntary sacrifice atones for all his crimes. Kipling will add one or two more meditations on this theme in his later, profounder work. For Mrs. Bathurst, Inspector Hooper will write an administrative report upon those two dead bodies by the railway line. We may hope that he will have the sense to forget the false teeth and write "unidentified tramps." A perfunctory enquiry, thick with meaningless verbiage, will conclude the matter and satisfy authority. Pyecroft and Pritchard, two honest men, have pronounced each his epitaph upon this man and woman, as do the doctor and Mulvaney in the earlier story. Mr. Kipling chose to immortalize them; four among how many millions unknown? The little episode of the friendly brook would have remained buried, spoken of in an undertone, over a beer in the pub, after Jim Wickenden's funeral, if a flash of genius had not determined otherwise.

Sergeant Raines and Larry Tighe, and "all India is full of forgotten graves." Warrant Officer Vickery and the "barmaid from New Zealand," and who needs reminding that South Africa is a land watered with blood? Jim—and Jabez, and Jesse—we can construct elegies in any country churchyard. Tales of crime in our everyday surroundings are three a penny. Hardly any come to more than a line or two in a police notebook. The odd one flares into an ephemeral headline, if it seems sexy enough to tickle prurience. Now and again an imagination fashions them into art, and a plain tale may illustrate the amazing diversity of creatures. Crime—as I have said and will repeat—is a mighty and perhaps the chief spring of illumination in the art of fiction.

✤

❧ *Raymond Chandler*

THERE IS A tale of a Zen master who placed a pitcher of water on the ground in front of his disciples asking them, "What is this object?" They made various suggestions, until one among them got up and kicked it over. Most of us see only with hindsight that this is the right answer. Nobody had noticed that the detective story was a cracked and leaky vessel that had gone too often to the well until Chandler in the 1940s gave it a kick and it fell to pieces.

To call an admired and cherished artefact worthless may take a clear eye, and sometimes courage; plenty of critics have that but remain merely destructive; they have nothing to put in its place. Raymond Chandler cannot be said to have reinvented the crime novel, which is as old as art and was flourishing all over the world, but he reinvented the "krimi," the tale of sudden, unexplained violence and the smell of fear. This he did in four beautiful books, up to but excluding *The Little Sister,* which begins so well and ends so badly. I also exclude *The Long Goodbye,* a competent work but over-laboured, lacking all spontaneity, and reeking of his own decline. He began late to write, after a long apprenticeship in magazine stories, and his disintegration set in suddenly. Four books is not a large output, but we are grateful to have them at all.

These remarks are controversial; they admit of and even insist upon some detailed discussion. Thus, merit for inventing the California private eye, as vivid and original a creation as Doyle's Holmes, is generally given to Dashiell Hammett, who indeed turned his own experience to good account in the invention of Sam Spade; he must have credit as the precursor. Without Spade would there have been Marlowe? Not in quite the same form, but we should remember that by the early thirties several of the "Black Mask" writers were already experimenting with this type of story, but only Chandler among them can be called an artist, and Hammett only survives in his shadow.

Hammett's trouble was more than being generally drunk and often dishonest; that can be said of many artists and indeed of the later Chandler. But he was a bad writer, lifeless and stilted in the fashionably monosyllabic Hemingway monotone that Chandler was to laugh at among the Bay City cops; unreadably mannered. One recalls Evelyn Waugh's mockery, "The imagination creaking, like old old corsets on a harridan." Some of Chandler's early prose, and more of his late work, does not escape this accusation: he wrote with difficulty, continually reworking, and only at his best is there true freshness. His early training in good plain prose, at Dulwich College, would be a help. His age was against him. Like his contemporary George Orwell he admired Somerset Maugham; not a good model but like Orwell his talent got the better of this pedestrian influence.

In his four central books he wears wings; a craftsmanly narrative technique learned in his short-story years is articulated into shapely prose delightful to read; accurate grammar and good syntax are not the least of his virtues. Into the anaemic, anaesthetised world of the detective story *The Big Sleep* arrives like a V-2 rocket. Try then to read a page of Dash Hammett, or other contemporaries. Try a page of *The Poisoned Chocolates Case* (published in 1936, vastly admired, even today described as "Golden Age," it is beyond belief arid, and written throughout in clichés). It is perfectly fair to let this stand for the hundreds of puzzle tales churned out in England and America in the two decades between the wars. With these handfuls of dust in the throat Ray's first book, in 1939, is like the drink Marlowe gives Lieutenant Breeze, the first sip a glimpse into "a better cleaner world." In those first two pages the dreadful house is alive, Norris the butler is—and very much so—alive, and as for Miss Carmen Sternwood, "thinking would always be a trouble to her" but by God she is alive. Marlowe himself, acting Doghouse Reilly, tempted to help the knight in the picture "who isn't really trying," or taking off his jacket in the sweaty greenhouse: this is that cold beer longed for after thirty days in the desert.

Chandler's own long goodbye would come only ten years later. A protracted topple into a big sleep, a hideously protracted farewell to all that was lovely. But in the meanwhile he had occupied the best seat at a high window, with a magnificent view, far and clear. (I'm well aware that this is cute, but in what words is one to map the pathos central to Ray's life?) His end is well known, thoroughly documented; one can only feel immense sadness at the horrible spectacle of publishers determined to wring one more bestseller out of poor moribund Ray, plying him with drinks and women while he "struggled with his goddam collar button." They were already naked in his bed, exactly like Carmen, some no doubt out of kindness and anxiety to please, others true harpies but all, inevitably, the praying mantis eating him up. Some were perfectly cold, like Mildred Haviland; others loved after their fashion, as Velma had, or Mrs. Murdock. But every one was a castrator. As beloved Cissy had never been. She was, she would remain, the only real woman. Poor Cissy—many cheap jokes have been made about her and I must leave her in peace without adding further vulgarities.

In the later work we can see the two sorts of castrator at work together. Mavis Weld keeps still some grip upon reality. "Believe me, I'm not worth it, even to sleep with." The little sister, after her marvellous beginnings, fades away and out of our ken, reappearing only to try to repair that plot "like a broken shutter." We are left with Miss Dolores Gonzales, her big tits and phoney Spanish accent, and phonier emotions; whether being seductive, serious, or frightened she is an outline drawn for a bad comic strip. The focus upon her is blurred yet further by Marlowe's realization that her femme fatale act is a cheap imitation: he is dazzled and hesitant just where he should be ruthless and his cynicism flakes off like her charm. There are "Hollywood" passages in this book written to heighten the effect of nervous tension, like that in which he waits for the phone to ring, with the "off-key neurotic charm" that was beginning to characterise Ray's own relations with the world and with women.

Worse was to come. Eileen Wade is both cold and cardboard, and about her there is something sweetly nauseating, like the incense added to the publicity fish-fingers, so that as well as being crisp and golden they will appear to be smoking-hot. Yet some have thought *The Long Goodbye* the crown of Chandler's career: it is the wreckage of his talent. The edgy, whiny note has become a self-pitying blub; neither Terry Lennox nor Roger Wade is anything better than Chandler-drunk, Chandler-impotent, the overpaid screenwriter turned studio-whore: both Paramount and Billy Wilder who had together made the marvellous *Double Indemnity* in whose script one can hear the authentic Chandler voice, deserved better than that. Reintroducing Bernie Ohls is nothing but a try to recapture the glow and verve of 1939. Howard, the publisher, is a tetchy mirror held to the too many Ray had known; Linda Loring is a wealthy harlot, the noun as boring as the adjective. Menendez exists only to say "Tarzan on a big red scooter"—the best-selling writer.

At the end of his life, in a sad little tale called "The Pencil," he would recall Anne Riordan. She is—alas—the first of his unreal women. For me *The Big Sleep* is his best book, since here only is Marlowe unsentimentally in control of his emotions. "Kissing is nice," he tells Vivian Regan, "but your father didn't hire me to sleep with you." I cannot avoid the suspicion that in the generally magnificent *Farewell, My Lovely,* after Anne Riordan's notorious "I'd like to be kissed, damn you," there was indeed a scene, perhaps pulled by sniffy Blanche Knopf, in which Riordan's knickers were taken down (as she deserves). How close an eye did Cissy keep upon these sloppings-over? It is a small flaw but vital; she remains a flat character because he was already sentimentalising her, as he would Linda Loring; whereas even with her skirt up to her waist he can stay detached from Velma's fatal fascinations. *Lovely* is full of marvellous things, and not the least that this is Ray's funniest book, but Anne Riordan sticks like a fish-bone in the throat; the weakness of her scenes acts like the tarantula on that slice of angel food.

The Lady in the Lake shows technical flaws. It is often wonderful. Mildred Haviland is more clearly perceived than Carmen, and she is the model for Barbara Stanwyck's throat-drying composition in *Double Indemnity,* the most frightening because the most convincing of his woman killers. She is not in the least sentimentalised: one cannot withhold sympathy and even respect for Degarmo. But the writing is oddly perfunctory. It may be because the book was so often interrupted; as the letters to Knopf make clear, Ray was pulled back in anxious, angry jerks. Kingsley is a poor stick and Adrienne Fromsett only there for the plot; she is lifeless and characters never directly met, Crystal Kingsley or Florence Almore, sweep her off the page—a pity because the book is full of good things, but too many of the jewels are set in lead rather than a silver sea.

The High Window—and how good these titles are—has the same feel, and probably for the same reasons, of starting marvellous hares which then escape. While a formidable craftsman tactically, a scene at a time, Ray was never good at the overall strategy of a book-length narrative. The reasons are not hard to find and are clearly expressed in his letters. To his friend Erle Stanley Gardner, author of the Perry Mason books, he is full of admiration for the seamless smoothness, the way "each page throws the hook for the next." But who now reads a Perry Mason book? They are long sunk beneath the wave and for this very reason: there is no grit at all in them, every situation and personage swallowed down like so much Jell-O. Chandler is always torn between his ability to draw character in a few lines (how instantly do Mrs. Murdock and Merle Davis come to life, inside that horrible house in Pasadena) and his uncertainty what to do with these wilful spirits. The "good plot" thought necessary to successful krimi-writing was a perpetual worry to him. He could see that a Perry Mason required a cast featureless and plastic, to be moved about in the mouth and masticated like chewing gum before being spat out and renewed. He could see in the most obvious of examples that a Dickens "plot" is a farrago of nonsense, so lamentably contrived that the sensible reader disregards it altogether.

In his California world he could produce ever-memorable people in three lines. *The High Window* is full of them: in the same building are the old coin-dealer, the cheap dentist, the worn-out lift attendant: "I'd change places with him. Even if he only got to Frisco and was pinched there." In the Bunker Hill rooming house are the pathetic young man in the straw hat, the carroty-haired manager Hench, his girlfriend—and they are all memorable, not to speak of the Pietro-Palermo Funeral Parlor. In Morny's nightclub we will meet the people who so conspicuously, in this same Idle Valley, fail to come to life in *The Long Goodbye.* The fifty-dollar joy-girls have been censored by the Hays Office, Morny himself and Linda Conquest are stock Hollywood scenery, but the barman is who we remember. The ineffectual Leslie, or Dr. Moss—these people are not mere chessmen to be jiggled about by "You and Capablanca" as Marlowe says, making faces at the mirror . . .

Seen in terms of plot, these disparate elements are stitched together with much narrative skill: the fabric remains loose-woven and bumpy; fine, but the author's anxiety to achieve a tight, smooth surface does not allow material to run freely off the loom. It is the most cannibalised of his books, with whole sections, like the old Jewish pawnbroker episode, lifted from the earlier stories which Ray thought of as ephemera, for was not *Black Mask* just a pulp magazine? The invention often wavers, the narrative plods, the writer seems often tired or distrait; by the end, Chandler would be obliged to find per-functory answers for a bundle of loose ends.

This conflict lodged deep in the writer's conscience, between the demands of plot and of character, winds up the spring: the tension allows us, fifty years on, to read and re-read these books with delight. Could one today get through ten pages of Perry Mason, even while waiting for one's flight to be called? I doubt it. But undoubtedly, these two books flare and sputter. They do not burn with the incandescence of the first two.

The uneasy feeling, that a writer this fine should be already on a downhill path, turns to sadness with *The Little Sister:* that opening page, of Marlowe and the bluebottle, was never excelled. Bay City, a series of brilliant sketches of the whole Santa Monica-Venice slide area, seems likely to excite us as never before. Consider the graffiti on the wooden hoardings, the little man who counts money in the kitchen. The optometrist and his toupee. That seedy hotel—and the cigar-counter girl, one of Ray's virtuoso touches; why should it all collapse so disastrously? When, and after an ominous lapse of time, we will come to meet Eileen Wade, the blonde to end all blondes, we will think back to Dolores Gonzales and this first great squirm of embarrassment. Her preposterous apparition ruins Mavis Weld and will eventually demolish the entire book. At first we suspect some trick, some parodic invention. The nipples and the cigarette holder should echo the anklet and the tight slit skirt of *Double Indemnity,* of Wilder's photography and Barbara Stanwyck's legs, but Chandler fails to catch the trapeze. "I wear black because I am beautiful and lost"—even in Hollywood, we ask, how could Ray pass so shame-making a line for the printer?

Reading *The Long Goodbye,* we realise sadly that there is nothing left of Ray but the sediment of alcoholic self-pity and Eileen Wade, a sticky mess of wet sugar in the bottom of a teacup. Ray himself knew it. "San Diego—one of the world's most beautiful harbours. But Marlowe has to get back and count the spoons." Ray is now a rich successful whore, and knows. *Goodbye* still contains good things: Mr. Harlan Potter drinking tea, the Sheriff rolling a cigarette one-handed, the Demerol-prescribing doctor; but these are too few to nourish a long, weary, and embittered book. To get rid of the sour smell of a burnt-out case we must turn back as far as *The Big Sleep*. For that was the good time, when Ray and Cissy were still poor but movie magnates could be laughed at. Indeed Bogart and Howard Hawks, undeniable big shots, could phone, worried; there seemed an anomaly in the script, hereabouts: what had actually happened? "I haven't the least idea," said Chandler. It had just . . . happened, from a moment notable in prose fiction, when the appalling house in Laurel Canyon Drive comes to life.

They crowd into our ken, insolent, pushy and pathetic: Joe Brody and the thigh-swinging Agnes, Owen Taylor and Eddie Mars, little Harry Jones who dies with such dignity. There is nothing like them, and there won't be. What does it matter, the how and the why? They are there to follow each his fate, growing out of that inevitability that cares nothing for artificial contrivance. It is Carmen who has brought all this about, and these others must follow, doomed by her search for pleasure. Agnes will drive off in the rain with four dead men behind her, and Marlowe will go to his rendezvous with Lash Canino, to save his skin only by the caprice of Eddie Mars' humiliated, manipulated wife.

I call it a masterpiece; one of the fundamental crime novels of history, and we don't have that many. Marlowe's instinct to let General Sternwood die with his dignity intact, like Harry Jones, in ignorance that his dreadful daughter has killed Rusty Regan out of vanity, unable to accept that she is not irresistible—this instinct is right, and generous, and has also something called nobility. No other writer will come to throw this perfect pitch of the California krimi. Ross MacDonald was a fine, a thoughtful, an elegant writer. Is it unfair to say over-derivative, that Chandler's long shadow covers his work?

One can have no doubt at all. Frilly, fluffy Cissy really was what he called her after her death, the beat of his heart. It is the case with many a famous writer and several instances come to mind; one could cite both Carrie Kipling and Jessie Conrad. They can be plain women, with more of character than charm, and can also be pretty and intensely feminine, as was Cissy: alas, she was too old, and became too ill, to keep the needed grip upon her wayward, fantasy-ridden romanticist. There exists a piece of paper, upon which Ray had sketched some very rosy future prospects. Cissy found it and added a postscript: "Raymio, you will come across this, and you will laugh at these splendid visions. Or, maybe, it will not seem so funny." It did not.

Marlowe stunned and hog-tied, awaiting death from Canino, can make jokes still, can say "Kiss me, Silverwig." And she frees him, on the gamble that he can match the formidable and sinister assassin: we can accept this. The killing of Harry Jones—"You ain't sick from just one drink, are you pal?"—is as shocking as anything in the genre, but one has faith in Marlowe because his focus has not yet been blurred. He will not give in to Vivian Regan. "Caterpillar blood," he jokes when she taunts him with his coldness. He throws Carmen out of the house, if need be "just as you are, naked," and she had better believe it. This unsentimentalised Marlowe will survive some years; asked whether he knows any tall blondes he will say "I hope so. How tall?"—we have still a way to go before the gluey flytrap of Eileen Wade. But it won't last. He will not walk in upon Mavis Weld in the bath—"not if it's that easy"—but all too soon it will be that easy and he'll be breathing heavy, on top of Linda Loring.

From the moment of Cissy's death there is little worth saying about Raymond Chandler, and little from his pen worth reading. But in the splendour of these first four books (there were only seven in all, and a handful of stories, but he was over forty when he wrote *The Big Sleep,* and Cissy sixty, and both worn) we may still recognise the freshest and most inventive writer of a whole American generation. Ray saw his own, his marvellous California from a high, high window; a splendid, sharp, beautiful, flawed and ignoble vista. And he fell out of his high window. It was not Mrs. Murdock who pushed him. It was Anne Riordan.

But before, he had seen a long way.

�֍

❧ Dorothy L. Sayers

IT WAS NOT a good year for Europe. For England, in particular, and there is not much to be said for English literature in this year of Mr. Baldwin's reign and Kipling's death. Of the writers then at work in 1935 who is read today? Greene, Waugh; a handful of the thirties poets, notably Auden. Shaw and Wells are remembered I suppose, if not much read. And if I have not cited Virginia Woolf or D. H. Lawrence, I suspect that they are always mentioned, but more seldom enjoyed. But who now recalls the great gurus of the time like Arnold Bennett or Frank Swinnerton? Would a name like John van Druten mean anything at all? In the memories of a few old men; a few faded copies in what that generation called "sixpenny bookstalls." One might cite Noël Coward as still funny: would anyone still think Edgar Wallace exciting? It is instructive to re-read George Orwell, who survives for clear thinking and plain speaking, and who put his penny on the survival of Somerset Maugham on account of the same virtues: he would have lost it.

In these years the writers of detective stories proliferated. They sold enormously, were thought intellectually respectable, and thought a great deal of themselves. They are all unreadable; the great thing was to devise a new exotic method of killing people and without the killer being at once guessed. Sixty years have passed and point to a paradox: two survivors of this time, constantly reprinted, are Agatha Christie and Dorothy Sayers. If the first is the darling of Hungarian students learning English, the second is re-read and loved. This phenomenon is often ascribed to snobbery, Lord Peter Wimsey being a pleasantly Woosterish figure, but the explanation does not satisfy me.

Gaudy Night is arguably, to myself evidently, Sayers' best book. Wimsey appears only in the second half. Indeed it is not a "detective story" and makes only a superficial pretence of being so: viewed according to those canons it would appear as her worst. Instead, it is a serious book, seriously written. Into it she put a great deal of herself, thoughts and beliefs as well as talent—it can even be said "too much"; it is, also, a longish book. A greater concentration is noticeable, of thought, and effort to express it: the writing is highly articulate and betimes over-talkative. It is the end of her crime fiction; the only subsequent Wimsey book she described as "a love story with detective interludes," a frivolous romp and a sop to popular demand. Thereafter she put her real skills to the service of religion, theology, and translating Dante.

Both seriously and well written, never a common combination; arguably unique in the crime writing of the twenties and thirties in English-speaking countries. Sayers had a good mind, academically trained, and was proud of her First in English from Oxford University. It came naturally that she should choose Oxford as the setting for this magnum opus: it was also a mistake, for she was anxious to exorcize psychological wounds, which add to the interest of the book but also and gravely mar it. She had never written seriously. She could afford to try, because she was by now wealthy, with a consider-

able reputation as an author of chatty, jokey books and especially for their popular protagonist, the Lord, but she was
nervous of her sales going down should she be "serious"; well
she might be. She attempted to blend two distinct genres, and
the patchwork is sometimes uneasy.

Wimsey reflects many of her own interests. Naturally, he too
got a First—in history, and at Balliol. He is a book collector of
eclectic tastes, a Latinist who speaks good French (his other,
and over-many, fictional skills need not detain us, here). He is
well bred, from an old family, and well-mannered, in the modern style of tact and sensitivity as well as in the formal elaborate
good manners of the Edwardian upper class, secure in many
thousand owned acres. Sayers valued these qualities. It is
something better than the commonplace snobbery of wealth
and strawberry leaves: we are told clearly that his brother may
be a duke but is beef-witted, and that his sister-in-law is a
bitch.

Her father had been Rector of a large East Anglian parish
and a distinguished classical scholar. She drew an enchanting
portrait of him in *The Nine Tailors,* generally seen as her best
book, since she combined a novel murder method with a vivid
and affectionate portrait of the fen country: this love and verve
make it a sunny, happy work of immense charm. But *Gaudy
Night* has altogether more profundity and resonance, and here
she drew back veils upon her own self. In this context her two
preceding books should be noticed. *Five Red Herrings* and
Have His Carcass are both alarmingly dull, conventional stodge
full of fingerprints and timetables, lacking all that Sayers knew
to be essential to any work of worth: character as a moral
pivot. She felt the spur to attempt an ambitious book, with life
in it.

She had introduced, a few years back in *Strong Poison,* a

character of vigour, struggling for life—in both senses—in a book otherwise undistinguished. Harriet Vane (who writes detective stories for a living) is a young woman of principles but by the conventions of 1930, loose. She is accused, upon technically sound presumptions, of murdering her lover. Wimsey believes in her, detects the real criminal, and in the course of doing so falls in love and asks to marry her. She refuses. Owing him her life she cannot make him a gift of it. This moral principle gives some solid grounding to an otherwise trite tale. Behind all the zizz and sparkle of *The Nine Tailors* there is nothing comparable to this pertinent point. Here a young woman has remarried on the reasonable assumption that her first husband is dead. He is still alive—but we do not care, for these personages have no life in them; our attention remains limp.

Harriet thinks of herself as damaged goods; she must not abuse generous instincts, must not palm off this devalued woman upon a rich and infatuated admirer. She asks for friendship, and Wimsey, unexpectedly human, lonely, with nothing in his existence but vanity and pretension, persists in asking for love. This uneasy and real dilemma is the position in the opening pages of *Gaudy Night*. A promising start. Instead of yet another murder—stale and flat as old herring—a moral tension, full of raw sensitivities and overstrained nerves.

Furthermore, the earlier book is of interest because Harriet is within a hairsbreadth of the death penalty. The judge, while admitting doubt over her motives for murder, is inclined to condemn her for "living with a man." The historical Mrs. Rattenbury was certainly in mind: inside many a chalky Victorian head was the preoccupation with sexual sins. Is fornication the first step towards homicide? However ludicrous it must now seem, that question killed Mrs. Rattenbury as surely as the hangman who executed her young, pathetic lover.

The self-portrait is barely disguised. A trial for murder is simply a dramatisation of a writer's flaring imagination, but Sayers herself had been "living with" a man, and though it was not widely known—the gutter press in the thirties being less given to prurient detection into private lives—she had a child. Sayers leaves us a small but distinct clue: Harriet likes to be known as "Miss H. D. Vane." Herself made always a considerable fuss about being Miss Dorothy L. Sayers.

Thank heaven there are no murders at all in *Gaudy Night,* although two are possible and appear likely. For we are left in no doubt; the author of these sinister goings-on is disturbed, gravely so, and these frustrations will end in physical violence focused upon a physical person. We have thus the ingredients for a thriller. Will it happen? The suspense is rather too lengthy but adroitly conveyed. It is at first no more than a question of anonymous letters, obscene and aggressive, addressed to members of an Oxford College, whose authorities are naïve enough to ask Harriet for advice, as an experienced writer of detective fiction rather than as a woman of sense and sensitivity. But "Shrewsbury" is Sayers' own college of Somerville, under the thinnest of veneers.

One does not resist the temptation to speculate. Could there in reality have been such an occurrence? Authorities would certainly have preferred to be discreet. Calling in the police was unlikely to be helpful. The woman adumbrated, clearly psychologically unbalanced, could so easily be one of themselves—Sayers handles this with skill. To suggest such a possibility was to skate upon very thin ice, but it could be argued that Sayers felt no threat of a libel action; for the publicity would be undesirable in the extreme. It is feasible, just, to suggest that the distinguished alumna, expert in detective procedure and familiar with the ways of a women's college at a time when these were not altogether greeted with joy by antiquated Oxford, might have been thought helpful to advise over this embarrassing small problem, as no leaden police officer could be. There are, furthermore, young girls in our care.

One must say at once that no evidence survives, to my knowledge, to suggest that this was in any way the fact. Much likelier is that some such occurrence took place elsewhere, that Sayers came to hear of it, was struck by how well it would fit into the enclosed garden of a women's college in the late 1920s, and could not resist a statement of her own ambivalent feelings towards Oxford.

This background is admirably conveyed. Blue-stocking ladies say "Great Scott!" and "Let's swoop down upon the ices"; there are splendid comic vignettes such as the Vice-Chancellor's unveiling of the clock; a wealth of descriptive detail gives a satisfying, vivid reality to the narrative. This world is still ruled by good manners: "The Dean's compliments to Miss Baker and would she kindly bear in mind the rule about visitors." It is consistently well-written.

Sayers treats it as the "locked-room mystery" fashionable at the time. Within this classical *hortus conclusus* the author of nasty doings could only be a servant (respectable, reliable women), a student (fundamentally unlikely), or alarmingly, a member of the Senior Common Room. This probability, given verisimilitude by the Poison Pen's use of a Latin quotation, provides Sayers with a theme of abiding interest, that of truth to oneself, integrity: a quality much in Harriet's mind. She, for Vane read Sayers, postulates a woman academic who has throughout her life put intellectual and moral standards ahead of her personal relations. Few of them married and fewer still had children. If such a woman, with responsibilities owed to the students under her direction, loyalties owed to colleagues—and to the cause actual then as now of women's rights and liberties—could be so far perturbed as to threaten the College's structures—there would be the devil to pay. The book is much enriched by this debate.

There are several allusions to a writer's "nasty propensity" to treat real happenings as episodes in fiction. I am much in debt to Barbara Everett, distinguished Shakespearian scholar and Senior Research Fellow at Somerville. She thought it unlikely, and I agree, that Sayers would have used raw material of this nature so openly and blatantly. (It is true that *Murder Must Advertise* is openly based upon personal experience, but this is another "merry romp" and could give offence to none.)

Everett found the undoubted subsequent coolness Somerville displayed towards Sayers both understandable and justified. The approach to Oxford was aggressive, vulgar. She could admire and enjoy the book, sharing my respect and affection for the writer, while disliking this trait in her character. I feel sure that this is an accurate view: Sayers could indeed be a vulgar bully. And much of it calls for forgiveness. A shy and timid woman, she suffered from a clumsy physique and chronic psychosomatic trouble with her hair. She was generous and kind-hearted, and loved Oxford with an over-sensitive passion; as often happens, these doggy affections, all bounding and licking, had the contrary effect to that desired.

Her fictional solution to the intrigue is contrived but will just scrape by. A woman has had to take a job as "scout," having been widowed by the suicide of her husband. He was a promising young academic whose ambition has led him to falsify a piece of research, a malpractice ruining his career. His suicide note (containing the Latin quotation) implies that he has been unjustly hounded by cruel and callous women. This largely uneducated young woman, who sees her job as making a home and bearing children (she has been left with two little girls), cannot comprehend the gravity of what in her view is a trivial malfeasance.

Here is the portrait of Miss Barton, feminist and "the best psychologist among us." As seen by a witness she is an "institutional sort of female, dressed in sackcloth, grey hair badly bobbed, earnest manner." Well, some feminists are like that today, and it could also be a portrait of Sayers in later life, "bloomers much in evidence." Miss Barton is kind-hearted and sensible in her approach. "Oh the usual thing, you know; morbid desire to attract attention." Some of these sketches may have guyed Somerville personalities.

Wimsey, called upon to investigate when Harriet's own psychological blockage obfuscates her powers of observation, makes short work of this minor problem. The male can separate logic from emotion, a notion women today will sniff at, and well they may. The book ends on a happy note with Harriet at last able to accept his offer of marriage; characteristic of Sayers they both take refuge in speaking Latin . . . Her emotions towards Oxford really had got too doggy.

Readers seem to have enjoyed this particular *aperçu* of the ancient university: there is a pleasant anecdote of a provincial couple visiting Oxford unimpressed by either academia or architecture. In some despair their guide paused in Catte Street to say, "Here Wimsey proposed to Harriet": they were moved, thrilled.

Noticeably, the Senior Common Room treats the unmasked poison pen with kindness and common sense. "Now don't say such dreadful things but come and lie down and take an aspirin." Today there would be three psychiatrists fussing round, before you could say Jack Robinson. The academic ladies have been frightened out of their wits, but there will not be pursuits or punishments, no malice toward this distraught woman. All women know suffering, and solidarity will prevail.

This is all very far from the average "detective story" of the period, which made do with eight or ten cardboard figures to provide "suspects," thought little of two or three murders to relaunch a flagging narrative (with as many flesh-creeping devices as ingenuity could invent), and never would a serious thought distract a reader from adamant superficiality. The facetious substitutes for humour, and sentimentality for pathos; nowadays, naturally, sex (in sticky truckloads) can plug every awkward gap, but not in 1935.

Whereas Sayers has nothing to offer but the aberrations of a disgruntled servant? A longish book is padded, at times outrageously, with ladlefuls of Oxford detail. Wimsey's insufferable nephew is allowed to parade notions of undergraduate humour not just tedious but culled from Ouida. It is true that Bunter's obsequious hoverings are kept to a minimum and only once does Wimsey say "Hullo-ullo," but it all sounds a parody of Edwardian Oxford: punts, parasols, and Parsons' Pleasure. The loving visions of the University as the last refuge of civilized humane values can only be called self-indulgent fantasy: it is as though a young man fond of hunting were to put on boots and spurs to read Surtees by candlelight.

Sayers flung herself into all her love affairs with this noisy crash. At the Detection Club she dressed up in a robe belonging to Chesterton and played with gusto at secret societies, like Simon Tappertit. The BBC, which was to publish her radio plays, cringed with embarrassment at her enthusiasms. Still, they learned what a good writer she was, and how thoughtful in her craft: respect and affection would outweigh exasperation. The central, passionate theme of *Gaudy Night* is that society gives women the stick and that to defend themselves, on either an intellectual or an emotional level, they over-react. Who will judge them?—a question still largely unanswered.

The quality of this book is perhaps seen better in comparison with two of the same genre; one from Sayers' hand, five years earlier, and one from ten years later, after the war, by Margery Allingham, a writer then highly thought of. *Documents in the Case* is marred by the self-conscious straining after novelty which so weakens the genre: to write a book in the shape of letters and memoranda is at best an awkward device. Sayers tries to meet it by making her central figure a writer, compulsive scribbler of comment and even dialogue, while two more characters are chatterbox "silly women." The crux rests upon a technical point: an organic chemical when synthesized shows a structural difference perceivable under polarised light. This is arbitrarily established in conversation between scientists upon moral and metaphysical questions, which interest Sayers, but the characters are too slight to support debate of this nature. It could be, and was kept for *Gaudy Night,* for Harriet (again, a writer), for Wimsey who has the taste and leisure for speculation, and for the Senior Common Room, where it would be appropriate.

The Tiger in the Smoke could be published with success as late as 1952, so unwilling was the lending-library public to abandon Edwardian notions of bourgeois comfort. It is deplorable trash, notable in perfect fidelity to the Sayers pattern of thirty years before. There is an aristocrat detective, Wimsey-and-pee, and a comic manservant far worse than Bunter, called Magersfontein Lugg. There's a kindly old vicar, and a red-haired beauty called Amanda from a Good Family. To sound Holmesian, there's a lot about fog; street musicians talking fake cockney; a Scotland Yard man, very tough but properly subservient to the upper classes; and a preposterous theatrical villain. Everything is "Rather Frightening," and the result is flimflam.

While there is grit in a Sayers composition, behind coy disclaimers about poison-in-jest. In the Fenchurch villagers, the copy-writers at Pym's Publicity, the Senior Common Room, are truth and wit. Even in her early work she can rise above cliché, as witness the lesbian nurse in *Whose Body*. In *Gaudy Night* is the mature mind reaching out towards Dante, and behind the sham Oxford is real crime writing. The theme of woman's truth to herself is as valid as it was to Ibsen. There is much good social observation of England between the wars. Not for another thirty years would ostensible crime writing reach this level.

✤

✤ Georges Simenon

"I⁣T WAS THE time of day when things have taken on a deeper colouring but without vibration, closed in upon themselves in the wait for twilight." Early Simenon and arguably the best; this indeed is my thesis: there is a freshness to the sensitivity. The famous "plain prose" has a bloom upon it. The writer's later work will be more profound but the price paid for experience is the loss of this immediacy. The sentence is perfect, wrote itself; the pencil would always be nimble but less instantly "right."

It is the opening to Chapter Nine of *Lock Number One*, among the most captivating, the most puissant of the early Maigrets, and my translation has killed the sparkle and the cadence. "C'était l'heure . . ."—this deceptively simple prose is notoriously difficult to render; no one ever wrote better French. One can look to Greene, the nigh-exact contemporary, for comparison of the manner as well as the matter. Greene will strike one then as the better writer, for the broader and more varied canvas, and for better theology: the agnostic theist turned and bit the hound of heaven. Simenon did not, because the stoic materialist chose not to try: the Little Saint would always say "Je ne sais pas." A better writer perhaps than Mauriac, excellent theologian and who wrote like an angel but

a Bordelais-bourgeois angel; it was for that he was given a Nobel Prize. The Liégeois angel was not, any more than Greene.
The Swedes, it was said, felt Calvinistically perturbed by the
shared devotion to blondes (it is true that in Simenon's case
anything would do that moved and was female). The allusion is
trivial, goes only to illustrate the compulsions that afflict good
writers; the locus classicus is Joyce's scatology. Kinship is the
understanding of the profoundest sources in the human being,
of love and longing.

Nearly all good writers are "crime writers," for this is the
area where those deep-hidden movements of the heart are seen
naked. Mauriac understood that, as Swedes apparently do not,
which is perhaps why their prize gets given to mediocrities,
and is a joke.

It can also be said that Simenon is inferior to Greene because he is much less funny as well as narrower in range. Still,
he is not just prolific: he is in every sense a considerable writer,
and here in a small essay I can only look at one small fraction of
that huge output, the half-dozen early Maigrets. I must also admit bias, for these to me were a strong formative influence, and
perhaps it is also special pleading, for I knew him hardly at all,
and yet very well (we shared the passion for eccentric hats).
"Damn him," complained a (shared) publisher, "you think
he's asleep, and there's nothing he's missed." Banal but exact.
An opening sentence, again from *Lock Number One*—"Looking at fish through the layer of water which allows no contact
between us, one sees them . . ."—it is the Bastille-Créteil tram
on the outskirts of 1930 Paris; one sees Charenton with those
incomparable eyes, alive like the fish, longtime immobile,
until the shimmer sets it into movement, abrupt as the sudden
dart of the Thirteen tram. Simple words, none wasted; each
tells: the spareness has not the lumbering, laboured gait of

Hemingway but is alert and vivid as a Schubert melody. "La truite se vagabonde . . ."—looking at the Seine, he has instinctively given his page the swirl and ripple of the river. Only the good ones do that; his effects were not contrived. At Liège one can see his manuscripts. There are no alterations. The printed page would scarcely vary.

Much has been made of Colette's editing of the young Sim, the "Take out all the literature." It was only an immature attachment to adverbs and adjectives and boyish fine-writing. His cutting is instinctive, done as he writes; the pencilled page has the fluid transparency so praised and prized in France, and so seldom achieved. The vocabulary is everyday, that of an educated man but straightforward, without Parisian artifice. The occasional raciness of phrase has a peasant directness. If the quay at Charenton is "empty and stagnant as an underwater landscape," it is not coral reefs in tropical seas which come to mind, but a northern canal. The dialogue is as unforced. There is no slang such as gives, for example, to the street-talk of Elmore Leonard, the worrying feel that it will be dated before one has finished the book: what seemed so fresh when written has the life expectancy of a plate of salad. His characteristic mannerism, the broken or unfinished sentence, is the way people talked in 1930 and do today. The bourgeois personages are given a more grammatical turn of phrase, such as use of the subjunctive, and his fondness for the rhetorical question, in French hands often so tiresome a device, is engagingly homely. "Had she remembered to turn the gas out, before going to bed?" There is never any risk of speaking in Alexandrines; the paragraph will not become a garden of beautiful thoughts. We went together to the market for vegetables (he was fond of this—in, of course, the Rolls Royce). "Cher confrère," with engaging formality, "cabbage d'you think, or cauliflower?"

The Yellow Dog dates from 1931. That, it could be said, is
the high-water mark of the English detective story. Simenon
has been reading these, as is clear from ephemeral collections
like *The O. Agency,* and is still experimenting, but his personal
style is already clear and nigh full-grown; all those Ches-
tertonian sleuths bedizened with eccentric adjuncts in the
tussle for novelty and notoriety find themselves beached from
our first glimpse of Maigret striking a match: he is so very un-
flowery. Crime is the business of the police, men poorly paid
who worry about their shoes needing mending and the seats of
whose trousers shine; men often badly shaved and with dirty
fingernails; men who have come to work on a cup of coffee and
who will make frequent dives into the pub to keep going: they
have no time for proper meals and their teeth, like their digestion, are impaired. They have no traits of genius. What they
have is patience, tenacity, strength of character; they will stay
up all night at the crossroads because of the link which must
exist between those two odd houses and that garage whose
owner is over-glib and over-friendly.

Maigret, at the start of *Liberty Bar,* is lost, adrift and humiliated; it is much too hot and his clothes are sticking to him; he
knows nothing, and has been told to avoid scandal; he wanders
aimlessly under the blazing sun, wishing everybody would stop
gabbling at him. William Brown, who was so alive, is
dead . . . (Who cares, Edmund Wilson would ask exasperated,
who killed Roger Ackroyd?—who never had been alive.) Two
harridan women ran away, attracted police attention, and
Brown was found stabbed: from this "one line in the local paper" Simenon has built a beautiful book. After seventy years
the glow upon it is unspoiled. William Brown, who has known
every pleasure that wealth can bring, found his one remaining
happiness in the company of fat Jaja, and we can be reminded

of the famous lines Shakespeare wrote for Mistress Quickly upon the death of Falstaff, for fat Jaja is there too.

Maigret's celebrated first appearance in northern Holland is wooden and awkward. While one can admire the young writer's rising to the challenge of a police enquiry where he does not even speak the language, the characters are too slight to merit attention. The two adventures in Liège, fantasies from the writer's boyhood, have no real purpose, one might guess, but to shock the self-satisfied citizenry, and to try out the method.

But *The Yellow Dog* is a landmark in crime fiction and deserves close attention. Here Simenon is still bound by convention. The suspects are gathered together in the last chapter for the formal disclosure of the villain, clumsy device of the weary old whodunnit. There is the usual perfunctory use of surprise; the false clue and the faked murder-attempt: in fact all this could be another "Mysterious Affair," desiccated as though from the pen of Ronald Knox and set for novelty in Concarneau instead of Styles. Maigret's presence has the usual arbitrary justification: the Paris police officer is reorganising the PJ in Rennes—we must hope they were grateful. The book is thus miching mallecho throughout and not even well done, since the author is bored by the necessary bullshit. Why, then, should it be so good a book?

In alphabetical, I think also in ascending order, then; first, for atmosphere. Conan Doyle is praised and rightly for the evocation of Victorian London; the smells of leather, coal-smoke, and horseshit, of fusty clothes and fresh newsprint, of tea, tobacco, and chamber-pots—the river was still the open sewer of Dickens' day. Arguably our enjoyment of this is half sentimental romanticism and half imperial self-indulgence, but Doyle still writes admirably well. In the same economical phrases Simenon has done something a little more difficult; he has made a Breton fishing village "his." This in 1930 was utterly unfamiliar ground, as remote from Paris as Timbuktu and the local people as primitive and superstitious as in medieval times. I should know; at exactly this moment I was a child of three living in Le Croisic. Concarneau today is just up the road and was then in another continent, while in every respect identical.

This setting is formidably exotic, while the detective stories are of the utmost banality; in every picturesque village from St. Ives to the Orkneys, fat, or blind, or lazy (always eccentric) detectives were solving the local constabulary's puzzles at a shocking rate. Simenon has some fun with a young policeman's worries about correct procedure, and more with a gang of imbecile journalists. "Terror Reigns in Concarneau!"; it is Corker and Shumble, hoping for a scoop. The facetious and even the satirical detective story were to become established subspecies but this is not his intent: terror does indeed exist, but a nastier sort and for blacker reasons. From the first paragraph this is a book of startling force and freshness. No writer outdoes this vivid impact, nor the economy of phrase to convey it. The sounds and silences in the Café de l'Amiral are instant magic; every detail of the mayor's house, the beach, the streets of the old fortified town become an incantation. The reader watches under compulsion, shivering in the draught. This on any terms is fiction at a high level.

Second, for character. From the moment we glimpse flat-chested Emma, adding up her accounts at the cash desk, we are riveted. Maigret sees her at once as the centre of the intrigue and we accept this without question, for the plain, sallow slavey is a striking portrait; a study but a fine one for *La Marie du Port* a few books further. There is not much plot in a

Simenon. It is perfunctory, fodder for the reader whose imagination needs support, but character is drawn in spare lines as on a sheet of copper, "placed" in the composition, formally, as a hostess places her dinner table. He will give us enough of the lighting, the flowers, the silver; he will tell us the menu (food is of much importance) but will then let character speak for itself.

Last, for what can only be called metaphysics—the quality necessary to crime writing, central in Greene or Mauriac as it is in the Russian masters or in Ibsen, conspicuously lacking from the detective story. The objector would instance Chesterton: why there does it sound so arbitrary, self-consciously artificial; and why above all is it dressed in such garishly written prose? The handling in these early books is still crude and uncertain, with heavy melodramatic nudges (a few more violent deaths, thought of as de rigueur to help the action along). Some of these first-period Maigrets are frankly dull; one does not get much stimulus from *The Saint-Fiacre Affair* or *The Crime in Holland.* But here, and in *Liberty Bar* and *Lock Number One,* is already the urgent questioning about the human soul: the nature of crime, the meaning of suffering, the effort toward redemption. In the earliest serious work is a rejection of traditional Christian answers. The theological pattern of Greene or Mauriac is discarded, and always he will ask himself whether he was right to do so.

Throughout his life he saw himself as a doctor, the good clinician sure that the right blend of exact observation, skilled analysis, and brilliant intuitive synthesis would give the right answers. Along with the intense awareness there would have to be the right mix of physical and psychological balancing. As late as *The Little Saint,* when he would write "Got it at last" across the jacket, he felt sure that the answer was within his grasp. Here, at the beginnings, is his reaching out towards the "meta" dimension, the barrier that neither physicist nor bio-chemist could penetrate but to which the major artist can come closest. He would refuse to theorise, for fear of emotion, of sentimentalising his mighty gift. This excellent research scientist will not allow himself to predict. But the best do predict.

Redemption will be admitted in that astonishing book *La Neige était Sale* (an untranslatable title; "Sullied Snow" sounds merely mawkish). Time and again as in *Letter to My Judge* he will come close, but the leitmotif of *The Little Saint* will be "I do not know." And that subsumes "Nobody can." The burden laid upon the artist is just too great.

Look, again, at the well-known facts of this life. Born in Liège, exactly where the French river Meuse becomes the Dutch Maas; of a Wallon father and Flamande mother. As a young man he travelled widely, and he spent the war years in the United States. To my view none of the African or American books stay in the mind. Simenon country is narrower than Greene's; stretches from northern Holland to the Vendée coast, to the island of Porquerolles, but will never touch Germany or Italy, Spain or England. French writers (save always Stendhal) are immovably hexagonal, and imagination will truly flare only when their feet are buried in their own soil: beyond France only Belgium and Holland answer this atavistic need for his place, inherent in his intensely physical response.

A Simenon book is saturated in climate and weather, in the tactile sensual grip upon street, pavement, house, the sounds and smells of interior structure and furniture; creak of staircase, humidity of stone flags, mustiness of cupboard, dust in the fold of curtain. The nature and quality of the light: this painter, so Belgian and also so Dutch, tastes the texture of rain or the dust motes in a sunbeam, for metaphysically this is all bound together. The life of the stone, the tree, is also that of man. In the child the apprehension is strongest and the adult Simenon would always remain the marvellous child of the Rue de la Loi. The intensity of this physical need extends to food and to drink, and of course to women, who are eaten rather than slept with. He must touch, smell, explore; hunger becomes frenzy; his girls were chewed up and swallowed. Landscapes are devoured and writing is a process of digestion. In Racine's terrifying phrase he is "tout entier à sa proie attaché."

Obviously, this is pathological behaviour. It is a truism to say that the behaviour of most major writers generally is pathological, and to point to Dickens or Dostoyevsky; one can say the same of Evelyn Waugh, who was not a crime writer. It is striking that Simenon formalises the patterns of his mania. His numerous doctor characters are all extensions of his wish to examine, to understand, and to diagnose. Doctor Paul, the famous police pathologist of the twenties, who chain-smoked as he worked—and gave his name to a dish still to be found on the menu at Lapérouse—was an abiding major influence, and it is no coincidence that Maigret's only close friend is Dr. Pardon. He was to carry it further. Mr. Jekyll and Dr. Hyde are interchangeable, and each time he writes a book (he would take his blood pressure at the start) he will inject himself with his special, highly toxic magic drug and die in a painful spasm: he would come to say that the books could not be longer because his own physique could not support the strain. Several of his characters give way to bouts of alcoholism called "novenas" (and notably in *Pedigree,* the account of his own childhood said to have been written when a mistaken diagnosis led him to believe his own days were numbered).

It is impressive, this immense and sustained effort to pass the barriers. It would end in great unhappiness, defeat, and the refuge behind the armour-plated legends created around the personage of the world's best-selling fiction writer. It starts so well but it does not progress.

> *Myself when young did eagerly frequent*
> *Doctor and Saint, and heard great argument*
> *About it and about: but evermore*
> *Came out by the same door wherein I went.*

This notoriously facile piece of verse, which was to acquire so great a sentimental reputation in late Victorian times, is oddly apposite.

It is rare for a writer's early work to be better than that of his maturity, though it often happens that it is the most admired. Much of Simenon's later writing, belonging to the forties and fifties, is among his finest, but this cannot be said of the Maigrets. They became pot-boilers, taken on to please publishers and to nourish the bank account. The colossal readership came increasingly to rely upon and to demand more of Maigret. The pipe and the gun, the patience or the anger; these are cheap effects, thin and perfunctory, relying upon technical brilliance and experience, and the stoop of the falcon becomes a querulous hunt after butterflies. The Maigret of the twenties, that of the bowler hat and the velvet-collared overcoat, the coal stove and the open platforms of buses, is the real one—just as the Paris of *A Man's Head* is the real one, that of the Santé prison yard and the Coupole bar. (It is mine too though I was barely in time, around 1950, to catch the last, the sunset glow.)

The "phenomenal" writer no longer exists and we would look around in vain for a Balzac or a Dickens. Perhaps Simenon is the last of these comets. Everything he is or does from the beginnings in the streets of Liège bespeaks the prodigious: great talent; ferocious energy; immense appetite. The comet whirls on for he can never stay still; whipped on and tormented by mighty compulsions.

Simenon was robust, as he had need to be, and lived to be old. When the uneasy millionaire comes to rest in Switzerland he is still a greatly impressive figure. He will ride the crest of this big wave until at last it breaks in age with the suicide of his too-greatly loved daughter, and then it shatters utterly. His guilt in this tragedy consumes him until all that is left is a little old man, quiet and almost shy, a *petit vieux* of rural France— gradually dwindling, bitterly unhappy, unable to die.

✣

❧ *Apologia Pro Vita Sua*

IT IS THIRTY years since the outset of my writing life, when fame and fortune appeared, hovered. These are fine things; to many artists they never approach. The accepted wisdom is to seize with both hands while the going is good. Shakespeare's sententious little phrase about the tide in affairs: one must feel the wave build, and surf on it. After a successful first novel the second is notoriously difficult; mine was effortless. Contracts shower in by every post, movie people invite one to lunch, journalists scratch at the door: the gateway has opened to the sweet life.

To reject this glad confident morning is great foolishness. Yet reject it I did, against much excellent advice, without understanding of motive and certainly without conscious reason. It is natural that I have thought much since, with many moments of regret and bitterness; bad since both lead to self-pity. But after thirty years one should have understood. This too is the lapse of time in which a reputation suffers eclipse before—sometimes—finding a truer level. The very young think their times exciting and that these will last: journalists like to count in decades and speak with contempt of the sixties when they were not born, unaware of the derision which in the following century one will attach to the nineties.

Most of these motives were psychological: the circumstances of my parentage, birth, and upbringing were such that I did not see the sweet life as it is led in literary London to be at all attractive. I do not intend to speak of my childhood; exasperated reviewers of autobiography complain of these long and self-indulgent accounts, all Muswell Hill and Aunt Doris. My parents were interesting, but that is for another time, another place. It is enough to say that the flat in a Georgian square, the joining of clubs, the reviewing for papers, the attendance upon parties, held for me no appeal.

But there are other reasons. These I have learned to call metaphysical. Most of us can find milestones in existence, a few well known and obvious (they intrude upon memory in the borderland between sleeping and waking), others discoverable, when a small happening, joy, fear, or shame, was seen to have a meaning out of proportion to its importance. It creates a shock wave; it bears upon the courses of decision, sometimes irresistibly, as when we put our elbow on the table, clasp hands to try an arm-wrestle, find ourselves bent. We know, occasionally, that it had to happen, that it was meant.

Crimes happen this way. Think, with any honesty, and we will all find moments when we were guilty of crime. Probably undiscovered and almost certainly unpunished; very likely nothing enumerated in any penal code. Nonetheless a milestone. The very word *metaphysical* (so poorly defined by the Concise Oxford Dictionary) appears too pompous: words like "moral," "ethical" (vague in the sixties, in the nineties nigh meaningless) impossibly sententious. What did you do then, kick the cat? Possibly; I once asked a peasant neighbour to kill a young pine marten I thought rabid. He did so with a stick. I could not do that, but ordering it done was worse, and in the end more grievous, more damaging, more dehumanising.

The point of metaphysics is that the rational approach is bound to fail. Even the laws of physics are thereby disrupted. The inexact, the social or behavioural sciences go haywire. Try it out at three in the morning—what Kipling called "the bad time when the cattle wake for a little."

I wrote my first novel without any idea of "crime." It had been purely instinctive (as most first novels are). I was surprised, even disconcerted, to hear a skilled and experienced publisher tell me it was a crime novel and that I should write two more for him. Quickly. The second was obediently deliberate; the third and fourth accidental—and that, tiresome Victor Gollancz decided over lunch, must be pseudonymous: I was deviating, annoyingly, from his view, formed in the twenties, of what crime fiction should be like. I found myself hating the crime novel, which seemed a silly and trivial concept, and so it is. But I had been given, technically, the label, stamped upon the famous yellow jackets. It would take me twenty years even beginning to grasp how to get rid of it. It took me that long to recognise that "crime" is indeed the key, but that my instinctive refusal of a reputation among detective-story writers was as right as it was inevitable. Ten years later it would be another brilliant publisher, Jamie Hamilton, who would lose his temper with me for "killing the detective." This one cannot do. This one does not do. No, but I already had.

The path is harsh, then. The search, for the harmonies of the metaphysical world, is painful. It demands unusual qualities of courage and perseverance, a fact most discouraging to myself. It exacts physical endurance and indifference to comfort, which makes it no easier. This world is visible and tangible in the simplicities of the natural world; in tree, leaf, and stone; is most accessible in mountains, and at sea, where both Conrad and Melville found and described it. The searchers are thought mad, at best dangerously eccentric and preferably avoided. Their own dislike of crowds, noise, and every vulgar demonstration compounds the problem. They are distrusted, and disliked. The natural consequence is that they turn still further from the crowded paths; relief comes with solitude. The man like Gérard d'Aboville, who has crossed both the Atlantic and the Pacific by rowing, does not take kindly to the press conference.

A further handicap is that the traditional "male" qualities of logic, reason, and structure are hostile to a world that defies analysis: the ugly word *destructured* has crept into today's jargon. Women are much better at metaphysical exploration, a fact vexatious to most men. The strongly feminine streak is noticeable in nearly all artists. For the male artist finds himself placed, uneasily, between the two worlds. His job is to try and join them. He cannot, of course, but his instincts force him to make the attempt to convey, to illuminate—isn't that it, to shed a little light? Rarely, and imperfectly, will he get anywhere. The painter or the musician is closer to the male world and finds a mathematical structure for his harmonies: whereas the writer, at sea in the maddening imprecision and opacity of language, struggles for toe-holds in a feminine, matriarchal universe; his frequent sexual inversion that seems likely to help him will prove to be a bitter disillusion. He will call also largely upon the help of the artificial paradise, and that's no help either.

From the beginnings of written art—a latish development, since so much weaker than other graphic arts and made still more diffuse by all those damned languages—"crime" shows as the most potent of themes. Whether theological, treated as mankind's disobedience to God, revolt and defiance; the expression of his impotence and frustration; or, as we would prefer to see it today, a pathology of the spirit, similar in nature to the pathologies of cellular biology, it has a universal fascination. Transgression and atonement, endlessly repeated in every permutation; it can be seen as mankind's rage, hatred, and longing for a world of truth and honour, where at long last peace, justice, and happiness would be attainable. For on that one point every philosopher concurred: the world is inescapably evil.

Painting and music, sculpture and architecture, we can see as mature arts. Mankind had practised them from the beginning. For the poorest and most primitive of peoples these arts were delight—relief from the harshness of existence, and a noble effort to out-run it. Great cries of longing for the unattainable. Within a shared language, poet and playwright joined in the cry of love and joy. And for the humblest of people in the poorest village, there was the storyteller, the entertainer, who placed these same themes in simple homely terms and language: it is from them we derive prose fiction, but it is not before the eighteenth century that we find this art developed and articulated in the modern sense of a bundle of paper to be printed and distributed beyond the medium of word of mouth. We are the poor relations, among artists, and today only two centuries after our beginnings we ask whether our day is not already run.

But we have served some purpose, for in no other art has there been this sustained enquiry into the nature of human behaviour. What is crime, and why can we never be free of it?— quite as cogent a question as at the beginning of the nineteenth century.

Do I sound in danger of asphyxia, from an attack of the academic solemnities? I should hope not, for a developed sense of the ridiculous is essential to the meta-world. Materialism to be

sure can be characterised by absence of humour, and so can
the false mystic and every guru, of whatever persuasion, who
rattles the collecting box. Popes, dictators, professors of economics, politicians, or tax collectors: all take themselves very
seriously, appalled and even much vexed by anyone daring to
see them in another light. Laughter distinguishes man from
beast; could I call it a meta-virtue? Don Juan, the Mexican sor-
cerer, is remarkable for an articulated and sophisticated system
of metaphysics, but still more for an outrageous sense of humour, and there is nothing he enjoys more than to deflate his
earnest young student of anthropology with demonstrations of
sheer farce: indeed the more serious the purpose, the more
preposterous the means. I do not think it in the least extraordinary that so much good crime writing displays this quality. So
do highly metaphysical poets—Auden comes to mind. Do we
like to think of ourselves in England as especially gifted at
using laughter to underline the serious? Some truth in that,
surely, but it's not a monopoly. The fictional murder in
Nabokov's *Lolita* is utterly horrible because it is so richly
comic—but hardly anyone noticed that this is a crime novel, a
very fine one. Lampedusa's *Leopard* is crime fiction in only a
subliminal sense but at its best—and funniest—when the author's eye rests upon Don Calogero Sedara. It is a mistake, as
Norman Lewis saw, to think of the Mafia as merely dreadful.
The real horror is the great funniness.

Of these writers cited, whom I think of as having altered my
life—and how many millions of other lives—only Kipling, I
think, has not used laughter as a necessary element in crime
writing, and this perhaps because laughter to him occupies a
special and distinct place in the world, a magical incantation to
be used when the world appeared at its blackest. This is so daz-
zlingly powerful a writer that the flaw is a minor one, but I do

believe that it diminishes him, for when he does allow his elaborate and detailed sense of farce to mingle with other themes, the result is unhappy. "The Village that Voted the Earth Was Flat" is enjoyable and even fascinating reading, but I see it as one of his flagrant failures, for on political themes he lost his sense of balance.

I am brought back, inevitably, to my times and to my self; the first more interesting than the second. When in 1961 Victor Gollancz told me that I was a "crime writer" he meant something very different to the major writers who have been the subject here of comment. He was relying upon the detective-story writers, who were the jewels in his crown, and he saw me only as a new and fresh variation upon the tradition. But if I was some years ahead of convention in this field— scarcely a merit, since the convention was thirty years behind—other writers thought as I did. I am not about to break a rule that I have no comment to make upon any living writer, but crime fiction, in the years between then and now, would break a lot of fresh ground. Vagabond and wayward writers would use as I had the conventions of the police procedural, the private-eye, or the district-attorney, which would condemn the antiquated notion that "crime" was a stilted, frivolous, slightly shaming genre that existed only to satisfy the public-library demand for a good light-read.

This is of course preposterous, and it is quite astonishing that there should still be reviewers specialized in facetious two-line descriptions of the "crime ration." Why not then a little rubric for love stories, for the "class" fiction the English are so addicted to; social promotion through adultery in Muswell Hill? The answer is simple enough: "crime" even at its crudest is more interesting and more readable than who-went-to-bed-with-whom. There are now a dozen—perhaps fifty—writers reviewed with respect when not with awestruck grovelling, who have used crime themes to give books of otherwise fairly humdrum merit some borrowed cachet. How many of these have employed the facetious (major standby of the "detective" writer in the thirties) as substitute for humour? How many fall still into the Edwardian gothic-and-gaslight with a sauce of glib psychoanalytical theory? How many still pander to those amazingly British nostalgias when the English were convinced of their intellectual, technical, physical, and especially moral superiority to other peoples? One may well ask.

*

I have used the "meta" word often and with dislike. It sounds awkward to the ear, looks pretentious on the page, contains little comfort. It postulates a world impossible to understand, escaping all rational description. But consider the world we have. In its physical dimensions what future does our poisoned air, fouled sea, and plundered land hold for us? Are we to withdraw to our last remnant of forest or mountain, there to sit like children on a sand-castle while the tide mounts? What are we to make of our moral world, corrupt at every stage and in every mechanism? Faxed or waiting-roomed, traffic-jammed or sleeping-pilled, how are we for an instant to sustain the illusion of freedom or decision? When we look in the glass we will no longer see the features and port of Renaissance man, the skilled hands and active feet, but the huge shapeless boots and clumsy gloves, the monstrously imbecile grimacing mask of Mickey Mouse. We are wholly owned by the Mouse Bank, mortgaged to the Mouse Insurance Company, manipulated by the Mouse Communications Corporation, and no, no, that isn't rhetoric.

It is a world uncompromisingly hostile to art. Mouse-art there is aplenty, and a sad spectacle it makes. But the artist bears witness to the degradation of our spirit, and plague-ridden, lice-infested Mouseman will not permit that. Throughout history the artist has forced windows open, held the door ajar, sought for light. That can no longer be, for the name of our world and its rulers is Fear. The artist must be howled off-stage, pelted with mouseshit, humiliated and crippled out of fear that some intolerable idea might contaminate the slaves shuffling along in lockstep; that the mousemask might be knocked askew.

It is claimed, and always has been, that nobody looks at or listens to the artist anyhow, so why bother? The argument does not move me, for a truth when metaphysical cannot be shaken. To say that $E = mc^2$, or that parallel lines even when extended to infinity will never meet, are truths in physics; in, say, a picture by Vermeer they are still true but not very relevant. That picture will tell us, instead, two other truths. One is that throughout history there have always been people who held the door open. Art has never failed; nor will it even now: the message is of hope.

The other is that man is not asked to solve a collective problem, but to take his individual responsibility. A fact consoling to the minor artist, only too conscious that he is not Jan Vermeer and never will be. Might I develop, a moment, that example? In that small but perfect collection, the Mauritshuis in the Hague, there are two Vermeers. They face each other in the same room, and either will knock one flat on one's back. But they are surrounded by a lot of good minor art, and one comes to realize that it forms a beautiful and a satisfying whole. I am proud and happy to think that without me, there would be no Stendhal.

A last word is needed; it belongs to my wife. This woman bore and brought up my children; when they became adult she asked what was left for her to do. She suffered bitter pain, upon the realization that the artist (at whatever level) is condemned to a solitary struggle. It was no mere fashionable feminism that led her to refuse this empty and impotent role of Comfort-Bringer, and she found herself bound to years of bleak and unrewarded effort. Independently, man and woman reached a hard-bought truth: the concept of "man" and of "woman" is meaningless. In the meta-world only the duality counts. Mrs. Vermeer is in the pictures and has no need to appose her signature.

Nothing is known of her. The novelist prefers it to be so; to know still less than I do of Saskia or Hendrickje. I can (as a painter would) arrange a few props and think about the lighting. He too makes preliminary sketches while the idea for a composition takes shape, and the writer (who enjoys craftsmanship) likes to spend time on priming a canvas. The squeeze of a (very) little paint upon a palette is thunderous with nervous tension.

One is conscious of this woman Dutchly banging about since "this floor is filthy." There is a smell of cooking cabbage and smoked sausage. One likes to see the windows washed—the light reflections will be the better. One makes a pounce. "Sit—there—get rid of the apron." A delay in getting the pose right. "The apron back on"; a technical detail. It must not be that washed-out blue: it shall be white.

The Daemon might at any moment appear. The features might not be these, familiar, rounded, Dutchly scrubbed. A face perhaps glimpsed in the street and now sharply present—why?—might arrive instead. The fresh smell of this woman, so often drawn while naked, washing with a tin basin on the floor, persists. "Stop fidgeting." "Yes but my sausage . . . I have to pee."

The novelist finds it difficult to paint this seventeenth-century Dutch woman. He knows about her clothes, her street, her vegetables, her pots, but what does he know of her mind? In church, bonneted, demure expression, is she thinking "What nonsense this man does talk"? Then as now, she knows much more philosophy than these bigots in black robes, but Jan might well say "Woman you better shut up, or you'll have us all in jail," for a woman speaking her mind would be labelled loose; heretical; in need of a good thumping.

She knew, and she cared, very little about politics, geography, history or economics, for hers was not a male mind. It is probable that her education went no further than to read, to write a clear neat hand, to add up her household accounts; but she knew all about the spirit. Books yes, she would read avidly, but she was a believer in oral traditions. As a child she spent many hours in stillness. She watched the hands of skilled men whose workshops were open to the street, she listened to old women whose experience was wide, she played with the children of the quarter, she knew many songs, and innumerable tales. Her own singing voice was true, and she could accompany it on a guitar. Ur-old knowledge was (we still use the expression) in her bones: an instinctive, pragmatic sureness of psychology. The liar, the cheat, the thief, the seducer, she could detect at sight.

She was of course free of all that paralyses us today; the floods of bogus information, smatterings of inexact science, the brainwashings of advertisers and politicians. There were many constraints upon her actions, but less angst in her thinking.

Upon Jan van der Meer, an unmeasurable influence; far

beyond his bed, his board, and "holding a pose." How much of this woman is in his eye and his hand?

She has characteristically annoying Dutch traits. The fearful obstinacy, the tactless bluntness, a dislike and distrust of intellect, a lack of imagination, an earthy hostility towards whatever might seem pretentious or posh. Art she rather dislikes (and paint smells, creates mess, takes up room). She puts up with it because she understands Jan's Daemon. She does hate the girls he drags in to sit; trollops all. Too many naked women and too much talk about the need art has of them.

Why does our knowledge of Jan Vermeer stop short? I do not try to write this novel. Certainly it is a crime novel, but I have too much respect for him and her both.

In these pages I have already asked the question which no biographer can answer: what Carrie Kipling, Jessie Conrad, meant to two very great artists. The pattern is everywhere different. Stendhal wrote immensely about his women: it is funny, touching, informative, and rarely his best writing; he felt dreadfully harassed about them all. Dickens' women were calamitous in his life and his art: they are his huge failure. For Simenon women spelt—and were—tragedy. And with his wife's death, Chandler disintegrates. What can one learn? Am I to "interrogate" (examples come at random) Véra Nabokov or Zelda Fitzgerald—or Mrs. Tolkien?

I shall maintain: the metaphysical nature of woman is the soul of art. I find nothing in the patterns of the homosexual artist (about which much nonsense is spoken) to contradict. The woman artist suffers today from social pressures as abundant as in primitive societies; let her then decide the question of whether she seeks a male complement to her talents. If we are to discuss the nature of crime, do we not find the seeds in the inevitable misfit between male and female? Surely it is our tragedy that we attempt fulfilment and so rarely reach it? Crime is the expression of longing and losing, and what else is our poetry, our music? We seek and do not find; upon this harsh condition we build our frustrations, our self-hatreds. The nature of crime is also the nature of art.

✣

About the Author

Called "the only major crime writer who can be classed with Simenon" (*The New York Times*), Nicolas Freeling was born in London in 1927 and spent his childhood in France and Southampton. He worked as a cook in several of Europe's grand hotels before turning to detective fiction in the late 1950s. His first novel, *Love in Amsterdam,* published in 1962, inaugurated the series of mysteries centered on Freeling's internationally-known creations, Dutch police inspector Piet van der Valk and his wife, Arlette. His 1974 novel, *Dressing of Diamond,* introduced his second world-renowned detective, the French inspector Henri Castang. In 1963, Freeling received England's Crime Writer's Award, followed over the next decade by many others, among them the Grand Prix du Roman Policier and the Mystery Writers of America's highest honor, the Edgar Allan Poe Award. To date, Nicolas Freeling has written thirty-two detective novels, including *Question of Loyalty, Double-Barrel, The King of the Rainy Country, Tsing-Boum, Auprès de ma Blonde*, and *The Widow*; a thirty-third, *The Sea Coast of Bohemia,* will be published shortly. He is also the author of two works based on his experiences as a chef, *The Kitchen Book* and *The Cook Book* (republished in one volume by Godine in 1991). He lives with his wife in Grandfontaine, France.

Criminal Convictions

has been set in Simoncini Garamond, a modern rendering of the type first cut by Claude Garamond (c 1500). Garamond was a pupil of Geoffrey Tory and is believed to have based his letters on the Venetian models, although he introduced a number of important differences, and it is to him we owe the letter which we know as old-style. He gave to his letters a certain elegance and a feeling of movement that won for their creator an immediate reputation and the patronage of François I of France.

Composed by The Typeworks
Vancouver, British Columbia, Canada

Printed and bound by Maple-Vail Book Manufacturing,
Binghamton, New York

Book design by Ken Wong